I0003277

NIST HANDBOOK 150-17
2011 Edition

National
Voluntary
Laboratory
Accreditation
Program

CRYPTOGRAPHIC AND SECURITY TESTING

Dana S. Leaman

National Voluntary Laboratory Accreditation Program
Physical Measurement Laboratory

April 2011

U.S. Department of Commerce
Gary Locke, Secretary

National Institute of Standards and Technology
Patrick D. Gallagher, Director

NVLAP AND THE NVLAP LOGO

The term *NVLAP* and the NVLAP logo are registered marks of the Federal Government, which retains exclusive rights to control the use thereof. Permission to use the term and symbol (NVLAP logo with approved caption) is granted to NVLAP-accredited laboratories for the limited purpose of announcing their accredited status, and for use on reports that describe only testing and calibration within the scope of accreditation. NVLAP reserves the right to control the quality of the use of the NVLAP term, logo, and symbol.

Contents

Acknowledgments

The editor wishes to thank the many colleagues that provided numerous reviews and contributions to the revision of this document. It is the author's opinion that these inputs have improved the overall quality and usefulness of the publication.

Foreword

The NIST Handbook 150 publication series sets forth the procedures, requirements, and guidance for the accreditation of testing and calibration laboratories by the National Voluntary Laboratory Accreditation Program (NVLAP). The series is comprised of the following publications:

- NIST Handbook 150, *NVLAP Procedures and General Requirements*, which contains the general procedures and requirements under which NVLAP operates as an unbiased third-party accreditation body;

- NIST Handbook 150-xx program-specific handbooks, which supplement NIST Handbook 150 by providing additional requirements, guidance, and interpretive information applicable to specific NVLAP laboratory accreditation programs (LAPs).

The program-specific handbooks are not stand-alone documents, but rather are companion documents to NIST Handbook 150. They tailor the general criteria found in NIST Handbook 150 to the specific tests, calibrations, or types of tests or calibrations covered by a LAP.

NIST Handbook 150-17 presents technical requirements and guidance for the accreditation of laboratories under the National Voluntary Laboratory Accreditation Program (NVLAP) Cryptographic and Security Testing (CST) Laboratory Accreditation Program (LAP), formerly known as Cryptographic Module Testing (CMT) LAP. The handbook is intended for information and use by accredited laboratories, assessor(s) conducting on-site visits, laboratories seeking accreditation, laboratory accreditation systems, users of laboratory services, and others needing information on the requirements for accreditation under this program. All statements in this handbook are supplemental to and do not contradict the NIST Handbook 150. If ambiguity unintentionally arises, the NIST Handbook 150 requirements shall be followed.

The 2011 edition of NIST Handbook 150-17 includes refinements from the various validation programs and eliminates redundancies between the program handbook and NIST Handbook 150. For historical purposes, the previous changes that were incorporated into the 2008 edition of this handbook were changes resulting from the release of the newest editions of ISO/IEC 17025, *General requirements for the competence of testing and calibration laboratories*, ISO/IEC 17011, *Conformity assessment—General requirements for accreditation bodies accrediting conformity assessment bodies*, ISO 9001, *Quality management systems—Requirements*, NIST Handbook 150, *NVLAP Procedures and General Requirements*, addition of new test methods, and editorial improvements. The requirements of NIST Handbook 150, the interpretations and specific requirements in NIST Handbook 150-17, and the requirements in program-specific checklists shall be combined to produce the criteria for accreditation in the NVLAP Cryptographic and Security Testing Laboratory Accreditation Program.

The 2011 edition of NIST Handbook 150-17 supersedes and replaces the 2008 edition.

The numbering and titles of the first five clauses of this handbook correspond to those of NIST Handbook 150. The primary subclauses in clauses 3, 4 and 5 (e.g., 4.1, 4.2, etc.) are also numbered and titled to correspond with those of NIST Handbook 150, even when there are no requirements additional to those in NIST Handbook 150.

This handbook is also available on the NVLAP website (http://www.nist.gov/nvlap).

Questions or comments concerning this handbook should be submitted to: NVLAP, National Institute of Standards and Technology, 100 Bureau Drive, Stop 2140, Gaithersburg, MD 20899-2140; phone: (301) 975-4016; fax: (301) 926-2884; e-mail: nvlap@nist.gov.

Introduction

NIST Handbook 150-17 augments NIST Handbook 150, *NVLAP Procedures and General Requirements*, by gathering the technical requirements of the Laboratory Accreditation Program (LAP) for conformance testing of Federal Information Processing Standards (FIPS)-approved and NIST-recommended security functions (e.g., cryptographic algorithms, security components, and protocols), and of cryptographic and security modules. Technical requirements are explained to indicate how the NVLAP criteria are applied to accreditation for conformance testing under the Cryptographic and Security Testing (CST) LAP.

Any laboratory (including commercial; manufacturer; university; federal, state, or local government laboratory; foreign or domestic) that performs any of the test methods covered by the CST LAP may apply for NVLAP accreditation unless prohibited by other programmatic requirements specific to the validation body. Accreditation will be granted to a laboratory that complies with the conditions for accreditation as defined in this document. Accreditation does not imply a guarantee of laboratory performance or of system-under-testing test data; it is a finding of laboratory competence and proficiency in conducting testing.

Testing services covered: Testing services include conformance testing of FIPS-approved and NIST-recommended security functions, of cryptographic and security modules, including module interfaces (and their interoperability), and of security policy compliance and management modules. For more information see the CST LAP's website <http://www.nist.gov/pml/nvlap/nvlap-cst-lap.cfm>.

Types of security functions covered: A security function is a part, a subset of parts, or the whole set of the Implementation-Under-Test (IUT) or System-Under-Test (SUT) that has to be relied upon for enforcing a closely related set of cryptographic procedures or security rules as defined in the specified standard and/or security policy. A security function can be a single cryptographic algorithm or a set of cryptographic algorithms, procedures or modes of operations that operate together to produce the output. Examples of security functions covered by the CST LAP are FIPS-approved and NIST-recommended cryptographic algorithms, security components, and protocols, as found in FIPS 140-2 Annexes (and all superseded and future versions), Personal Identity Verification (PIV) modules, automated vulnerabilities management modules, security policy compliance evaluation modules, and modules used in protecting sensitive information within computer and telecommunication systems.

Types of cryptographic modules covered: A cryptographic module is defined as a set of hardware, software, and/or firmware that implements FIPS-approved and/or NIST-recommended security functions and that is contained within the defined cryptographic module boundary. The types of cryptographic modules covered by the CST LAP are modules used in security systems protecting sensitive information within computer and telecommunication systems. These modules include, but are not limited to, hardware components or hardware modules, software programs or software modules, computer firmware or hybrid modules, or any combination thereof. For all cryptographic modules, the interfaces specified in each module specification are considered to be within the boundaries of the cryptographic module, and therefore are covered by the CST LAP.

Types of cryptographic algorithms covered: A cryptographic algorithm is a well-defined computational procedure that takes variable inputs, which may include cryptographic keys, and produces an output. A cryptographic algorithm can be a subset of a security function. The types of cryptographic algorithms covered by the CST LAP are either:

- specified in a FIPS-approved standard or NIST recommendation; or

- adopted in a FIPS-approved standard or NIST recommendation and specified either in an appendix of the FIPS-approved standard or recommendation or in a document referenced by the FIPS-approved standard or recommendation; or

- specified in the list of FIPS-approved and/or NIST-recommended security functions.

Types of security modules covered: The types of security modules covered by the CST LAP are automated vulnerabilities management modules, security policy compliance evaluation modules, and modules used in protecting sensitive information within computer and telecommunication systems. For all security modules, the interfaces specified in each module specification are considered to be within the boundaries of the security module, and therefore are covered by the CST LAP.

1   General information

1.1   Scope

1.1.1   This handbook specifies the technical requirements and provides guidance for the accreditation of laboratories under the NVLAP Cryptographic and Security Testing (CST) Laboratory Accreditation Program (LAP). It supplements the NVLAP procedures and general requirements found in NIST Handbook 150, by tailoring the general criteria found in NIST Handbook 150 to the specific types of tests covered by the CST LAP.

1.1.2   NIST Handbook 150 and this handbook constitute the collective body of requirements that must be met by a laboratory seeking NVLAP accreditation for the CST LAP.

1.1.3   The interpretive comments and additional requirements contained in this handbook make the general NVLAP criteria specifically applicable to the CST LAP.

1.1.4   This handbook is intended for information and use by all accredited CST laboratories, assessor(s) conducting on-site assessments, laboratories seeking accreditation, other laboratory accreditation systems, users of laboratory services, and others needing information on the requirements for accreditation under the CST LAP.

1.2   Organization of handbook

1.2.1   The numbering and titles of the first five clauses of this handbook are patterned after NIST Handbook 150, *NVLAP Procedures and General Requirements*, to allow easy cross-reference. The primary subclauses in clauses 3, 4 and 5 (e.g., 4.1, 4.2) are also numbered and titled to correspond with those of NIST Handbook 150, even when there are no requirements additional to those in NIST Handbook 150.

1.2.2   In addition, the handbook contains information in the annexes that supplements the text. Annex A (informative) lists the available types of tests offered by the CST LAP, and provides additional information and links to the CST LAP, NVLAP and NIST websites where the most current information and resources are located. Annexes B through E (normative) list additional requirements specific to the type of tests in terms of personnel proficiency, managerial and technical requirements, specific tools, quality manual, and other documentation. Annex F (informative) provides a list of additional acronyms.

1.2.3   The procedures and general requirements of NIST Handbook 150 and the interpretations and specific requirements in this handbook must be combined to produce the criteria for accreditation under the CST LAP.

1.3   Program description

1.3.1   The Cryptographic and Security Testing (CST) Laboratory Accreditation Program (LAP), formerly named Cryptographic Module Testing (CMT), was established by the National Voluntary Laboratory Accreditation Program (NVLAP) to accredit laboratories that perform cryptographic algorithm and cryptographic module validation conformance testing. As the LAP expanded in 2006 and 2007 and offered additional security types of tests, the program name was changed to Cryptographic and

Security Testing (CST). However, references on the web and in older documents from this LAP utilizing the obsolete nomenclature may still exist.

1.3.2 The National Institute of Standards and Technology, Information Technology Laboratory (NIST/ITL), initially requested establishment of this LAP to accredit laboratories that conformance test cryptographic modules under the Cryptographic Module Validation Program (CMVP). As the CMVP expanded, a new program, the Cryptographic Algorithm Validation Program (CAVP), was developed within ITL to encompass the validation of all FIPS-approved and NIST-recommended security functions. The CAVP became a separate program in 2003. Laboratory accreditation for the CAVP was added in 1995 as a component of the accreditation for the CMVP.

1.3.3 The CMVP is a validation program developed by NIST/ITL and administered jointly by NIST/ITL and the Communications Security Establishment Canada (CSEC). The requirements for this program are derived by NIST/ITL from FIPS PUB 140-1: Security Requirements for Cryptographic Modules or successors. The testing requirements are specified in the Derived Test Requirements (DTR) for FIPS PUB 140-1, Security Requirements for Cryptographic Modules or successors. Cryptographic modules validated by the CMVP are accepted for use in Canada and by the U.S. Government for the protection of sensitive, unclassified information. NIST and CSEC have developed an Implementation Guidance for FIPS PUB 140-1 or successors and the Cryptographic Module Validation Program document for cryptographic module vendors and testing laboratories. This is intended to provide clarifications of the testing process, FIPS PUB 140-1 or successors, and the FIPS PUB 140-1 Derived Test Requirements or successors.

1.3.4 The CAVP is a validation program developed by NIST/ITL and administered jointly by NIST/ITL and the CSEC for the validation of all FIPS-approved and NIST-recommended security functions. For every FIPS-approved and NIST-recommended security function, NIST/ITL develops a validation test suite for testing the correctness of a security function's implementation. Security function implementations that are successfully validated can claim conformance to the appropriate security function standard. All algorithm-specific test suites are bundled into the CAVP's Cryptographic Algorithm Validation System (CAVS) validation testing tool. The CAVP's CAVS validation testing tool is provided by NIST/ITL to those laboratories obtaining accreditation in the NVLAP CST LAP.

1.3.5 In response to the Homeland Security Presidential Directive (HSPD) 12 of August 2004, the NIST Computer Security Division (NIST/CSD) initiated a new program for improving the identification and authentication of Federal employees and contractors for access to Federal facilities and information systems. FIPS 201, Personal Identity Verification of Federal Employees and Contractors, was developed to satisfy the requirements of HSPD 12, approved by the Secretary of Commerce, and issued on February 25, 2005. Later that year, NIST established the NIST Personal Identity Verification Program (NPIVP) to validate Personal Identity Verification (PIV) components required by FIPS 201 within ITL. NVLAP added the PIV Test Methods to the CST LAP in April 2006. NVLAP accredits NPIVP laboratories to test PIV Card Application and PIV Middleware implementations for conformance to the NIST SP 800-73, Interfaces for Personal Identity Verification, which is normatively referenced from FIPS 201. The PIV objectives to validating PIV components by NPIVP are:

- to validate the conformance of two PIV components, PIV Middleware and PIV Card Application, with the specifications in NIST SP 800-73-1 or successors; and

- to provide assurance that the set of PIV Middleware and PIV Card Applications that have been validated by NPIVP are interoperable.

More information on the PIV test methods and the NPIVP validation program can be found at (http://csrc.nist.gov/groups/SNS/piv/index.html).

1.3.6 In 2007 the U.S. General Services Administration (GSA) requested that NVLAP add the test methods defined in the GSA FIPS 201 Evaluation Program (GSA EP) to the CST LAP, building upon NPIVP test methods for which laboratories had already attained accreditation. The GSA EP directly supports the acquisition process for implementing HSPD 12 by listing products that meet FIPS 201 and are interoperable with each other. The GSA EP requires NVLAP accreditation of the set of test methods referred to as GSA Precursor (GSAP) as a prerequisite for all laboratories seeking to become a GSA FIPS 201 Testing Laboratory.

The GSA EP was established to evaluate and approve products and services as compliant with specified FIPS 201 requirements and ensure product interoperability (see <http://fips201ep.cio.gov/>). As a prerequisite for all laboratories seeking to become a GSA FIPS 201 Testing Laboratory, the GSA EP requires NVLAP accreditation for the test methods listed as GSAP in this handbook.

1.3.7 In response to the Office of Management and Budget (OMB) Memorandum M-07-18 of July 31, 2007, the NIST/CSD initiated a new program for validating the implementation of the Security Content Automation Protocol (SCAP) standards within security software modules. To meet the needs defined in the Memorandums M-07-11 and M-07-18, NVLAP established the accreditation of SCAP conformance testing laboratories in December 2007.

The SCAP enables automated vulnerability management, measurement, and policy compliance evaluation; enumerates vulnerabilities, misconfigurations, platforms, and impact; and provides machine-readable security configuration checklists. SCAP is composed of six open standards:

- Common Vulnerabilities and Exposures (CVE) – a dictionary of security related software flaws;

- Common Configuration Enumeration (CCE) – a dictionary of software misconfigurations;

- Common Platform Enumeration (CPE) – a standard nomenclature and dictionary for product naming;

- eXtensible Configuration Checklist Description Format (XCCDF) – a standard XML for specifying checklists;

- Open Vulnerability Assessment Language (OVAL) – a standard XML for checking the machine state; and

- Common Vulnerability Scoring System (CVSS) – a standard for scoring the impact of vulnerabilities.

For additional information regarding SCAP see the program website http://scap.nist.gov.

1.3.8 Information regarding the most current additions, enhancements and extensions to the CST LAP types of tests at the time of this publication can be found in the annex associated with the specific test methods.

1.3.9 NVLAP reserves the right to expand the CST LAP and offer to interested laboratories additional types of tests not listed in this handbook. Laboratories are advised to review the CST LAP's website for the most current information (see http://www.nist.gov/pml/nvlap/nvlap-cst-lap.cfm).

1.3.10 All of the cryptographic and security testing performed under any of the CST LAP programs (e.g., CMVP, CAVP) are handled by third-party test facilities that are accredited as Cryptographic and Security Testing laboratories by NVLAP as described in this handbook and as described on the laboratory's published scope of accreditation. A laboratory's scope of accreditation will be published to the NVLAP website (see http://ts.nist.gov/standards/scopes/crypt.htm).

1.3.11 Figure 1 provides a generic overview of the accreditation process and the relationship between:

- the accreditation authority (NVLAP);
- the applicant laboratory (third-party laboratory); and
- the validation program (e.g., CAVP, CMVP, NPIVP, SCAP) as customer and technical requirements provider.

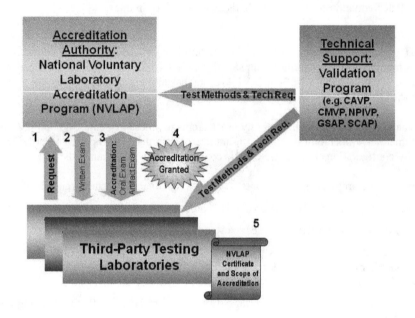

Figure 1. Accreditation process.

For a complete summary on the validation process, see the informative diagram in Annex A.

1.4   References

The following documents are referenced in this handbook. For dated references, only the edition cited shall apply. For undated references, the most current edition of the referenced document (including any amendments) shall apply within one year of publication or within the time limit specified by regulations or other requirement documents.

1.4.1   NVLAP publications

— NIST Handbook 150, *NVLAP Procedures and General Requirements*
   (see http://www.nist.gov/pml/nvlap/upload/nist-handbook-150.pdf)

1.4.2 FIPS publications

FIPS publications are issued by NIST after approval by the Secretary of Commerce pursuant to Section 5131 of the Information Technology Reform Act of 1996 (Public Law 104-106) and the Federal Information Security Management Act of 2002 (Public Law 107-347). For FIPS references specific to particular types of tests and/or test methods, see the annex associated with the specific test methods.

1.4.3 ISO/IEC publications

In addition to the ISO/IEC references listed in NIST Handbook 150, ISO/IEC references specific to particular types of tests and/or test methods are listed in the annex associated with the specific test methods. These may be purchased from http://www.iso.org,

— ISO/IEC 17043, *Conformity assessment – General requirements for proficiency testing*, 2010.

1.4.4 NIST Special Publications (SP)

NIST Special Publications (SP) in the 800 series present documents of general interest to the computer security community. The SP 800 series was established in 1990 to provide a separate identity for information technology security publications. The SP 800 series reports on ITL's research, guidelines, and outreach efforts in computer security, and its collaborative activities with industry, government and academic organizations. For NIST/ITL references specific to the types of tests and/or test methods, see the annex associated with the specific test methods.

The CST LAP website <http://www.nist.gov/pml/nvlap/nvlap-cst-lap.cfm> also provides a complete, up-to-date list of links to the Special Publications and validation program sites. The references listed on the website supersede the information provided herein unless otherwise specified. If no link is indicated, NIST Special Publications relevant to this program can be downloaded from the CST LAP website.

1.4.5 Other NIST publications and tools

See the associated annexes for test-specific descriptions of the Cryptographic and Security Testing tools relevant to the desired type of test.

1.5 Terms and definitions

For the purposes of this handbook, the relevant terms and definitions given in NIST Handbook 150 apply unless a term is redefined in this handbook. The definitions provided in this handbook are specific to the CST LAP, and when applicable, they supersede the definitions given in NIST Handbook 150. For a list of all acronyms, see Annex F. Additional test-specific terms and definitions are provided in the annexes specific to the testing. Test-specific terms, defined in other technical publications referenced in this document, supersede the definitions given in this handbook.

1.5.1
abstract test case
The specification of a test case that is independent of any particular implementation language.

1.5.2
accessibility
The assurance of continuous operation, continuous service or data availability of the referred entity.

1.5.3
approved
FIPS-Approved and/or NIST-recommended.

1.5.4
approved security function
A security function (e.g. cryptographic algorithm, cryptographic key management technique, or authentication technique) that is either (a) specified in an Approved standard, (b) adopted in an Approved standard and specified either in an appendix of the Approved standard or in a document referenced by the Approved standard, or (c) specified in the list of Approved security functions.

1.5.5
assertion
The statement or claim about the Implementation-Under-Test (IUT) that must be true for a cryptographic or security requirement from the governing standard to be met by the IUT. A cryptographic or security requirement may be expressed as one or more assertions.

1.5.6
authentication
Verifying the identity of a user, process, or device, often as a prerequisite to allowing access to resources in an information system.

1.5.7
availability
Ensuring timely and reliable access to and use of information.

1.5.8
confidentiality
The property that sensitive information is not disclosed to unauthorized individuals, entities, or processes.

1.5.9
configuration management
The management of security features and assurance through control of changes made to hardware, software, firmware, documentation, tests, test tools, and test documentation through the life cycle of the system.

1.5.10
conformance
The state of an implementation satisfying the requirements and specifications of a specific standard as tested by a test suite or an approved test method.

1.5.11
conformance testing
The testing of an implementation against the requirements specified in one or more standards.

1.5.12
cryptographic algorithm
A well defined computational procedure that takes variable inputs, which may include cryptographic keys, and produces an output. A cryptographic algorithm can be a subset of a security function.

1.5.13

Cryptographic Algorithm Validation Program (CAVP)

The Cryptographic Algorithm Validation Program administered jointly by NIST/ITL and CSEC. The laboratory's accreditation for conformance testing under this program is covered by the CST LAP. The NIST CAVP validation authority designs, implements, and maintains the Cryptographic Algorithm Validation System (CAVS) testing tool. For more information regarding CAVP see the validation program website: <http://csrc nist.gov/groups/STM/cavp/index.html>.

1.5.14

Cryptographic Algorithm Validation System (CAVS)

The NIST Cryptographic Algorithm Validation System tool.

1.5.15

cryptographic boundary

An explicitly defined continuous perimeter that established the physical bounds of a cryptographic module and contains all the hardware, software, and/or firmware components of a cryptographic module.

1.5.16

cryptographic key

A parameter used in conjunction with a cryptographic algorithm that determines operations such as: transformation of plain text data into cipher text data, transformation of cipher data into plaintext data, computation of a digital signature, verification of a digital signature, computation of the authentication code from data or shared secret exchange protocol.

1.5.17

cryptographic module

The set of hardware, software, and/or firmware that implements Approved security functions (including cryptographic algorithms and key generation) and is contained within the cryptographic boundary.

1.5.18

Cryptographic Module Validation Program (CMVP)

The Cryptographic Module Validation Program administered jointly by NIST/ITL and CSEC. The laboratory's accreditation for conformance testing under this program is covered by the CST LAP. For more information regarding CMVP see the validation program website: <http://csrc.nist.gov/groups/STM/cmvp/index html>.

1.5.19

Cryptographic and Security Testing Laboratory Accreditation Program (CST LAP)

The current name given to this LAP. The new nomenclature supersedes the Cryptographic Module Testing (CMT) LAP naming.

1.5.20

Derived Test Requirements (DTR)

Description of the methods that will be used by accredited laboratories to test whether the Implementation-under-test (IUT) or System-under-test (SUT) conforms to the requirements of the specified standards and the requirements for vendor information that must be provided as supplementary evidence to demonstrate conformance to the program-specific standard requirements.

1.5.21

GSA Evaluation Program (GSA EP)

The GSA FIPS 201 Evaluation Program administered by GSA. For more information see the validation program website <http://fips201ep.cio.gov/>.

1.5.22
Implementation Guidance (IG)
A set of documents published during the lifetime of the given standard that provides additional clarification, testing guidance and interpretations of the given standard. (Implementation guidance cannot change or add requirements to the given standard.)

1.5.23
Implementation-Under-Test (IUT)
The entity (e.g. the algorithm, the cryptographic or security module under test) defined within a cryptographic boundary that is the subject of the conformance testing and validation under the elected program.

1.5.24
information assurance
The practice of protecting and defending information and information systems by ensuring confidentiality, integrity and availability.

1.5.25
integrity
The property that sensitive data has not been modified or deleted in an unauthorized and undetected manner.

1.5.26
key personnel
The members of the staff that can perform a particular conformance testing task and who can not be replaced by any other existing laboratory staff member due to a lack of experience, knowledge, or credentials.

1.5.27
NIST Personal Identity Verification Program (NPIVP)
The NIST Personal Identity Verification Program established to validate Personal Identity Verification (PIV) components required by FIPS 201. The program is administered by NIST/ITL. The laboratory's accreditation for conformance testing under this program is covered by the CST LAP. For more information regarding the NPIVP, see the validation program website: <http://csrc.nist.gov/groups/SNS/piv/npivp/index.html>.

1.5.28
Personal Identity Verification (PIV)
The NIST initiative created in response to the HSPD 12 for improving the identification and authentication of Federal employees and contractors for access to Federal facilities and information systems. For more information, see the program website: <http://csrc.nist.gov/groups/SNS/piv/index.html>.

1.5.29
security
The assurance that a system will maintain an acceptable level of information confidentiality, integrity and availability.

1.5.30
Security Content Automation Protocol (SCAP)
A method for using specific standards to enable automated vulnerability management, measurement, and policy compliance evaluation. SCAP tools (systems) can be used by an end user (agency, corporation) to automatically evaluate the user's compliance to the targeted requirements (e.g., FISMA compliance, FDCC compliance). For more information, see the program's website <http://scap.nist.gov>.

1.5.31
Security Content Automation Protocol (SCAP) Validation Program
The Security Content Automation Protocol validation program administered by NIST/ITL. The laboratory's accreditation for conformance testing under this program is covered by the CST LAP. For more information regarding the SCAP validation program, see the website <http://scap.nist.gov>.

1.5.32
security functions
A part, a subset of parts or the whole set of the System-Under-Test (SUT) that is relied upon for enforcing a closely related set of cryptographic procedures or security rules as defined in the specified standard and/or security policy. A security function can be a single cryptographic algorithm or a set of algorithms, protocols, procedures or modes of operations that operate together to produce the output.

1.5.33
security requirements
Functionality and design controls which, when implemented in a system, facilitate information assurance.

1.5.34
survivability
The quantified ability of an entity to continue to operate or to survive during and after a natural or man-made disturbance, at a minimum acceptable level or post-disturbance functionality, and the maximum acceptable outage duration.

1.5.35
System-Under-Test (SUT)
The entity (e.g., the algorithm, the cryptographic or security module under test) that is the subject of the conformance testing and validation under the elected program.

1.5.36
test method
The definitive procedure that produces a test result. The test result can be generated by one test or by a test suite and can be qualitative (yes/no), categorical, or quantitative (a measured value). The test result can be a personal observation or the output of a test tool.

1.5.37
traceability
Interpreted in the CST LAP to mean that the conformance testing tool is traceable back to the underlying requirements of the provided normative standards.

1.5.38
validation
The administrative act by the governing Validation Program (e.g., CMVP, CAVP, NPIVP, etc.) of determining conformance of an implementation to specified standards and requirements (e.g., FIPS 140-2 or successor, FIPS 201-1 or successor) based on the review and acceptance of the test results from the accredited laboratories.

1.5.39
Version Control System (VCS)
The management of multiple revisions of the same unit of information (revision control system).

1.6   Program documentation

1.6.1   General

This handbook details the CST-program-specific requirements and technical procedures, while interpreting, detailing and expanding portions of NIST Handbook 150 for CST LAP use. Both the NIST Handbook 150 checklist and the NIST Handbook 150-17 checklist are used in conducting assessments in the CST LAP. Assessor use of the NVLAP checklists is to ensure that each laboratory receives an assessment consistent with that received by other laboratories. Checklists assist the assessor(s) in documenting the assessment to the NVLAP requirements found in NIST Handbook 150 and in this handbook. Checklists contain definitive statements or questions about all aspects of the NVLAP criteria for accreditation, and form part of the On-Site Assessment Report (see NIST Handbook 150). The most current version of each checklist is available upon request or on the NVLAP website <http://www.nist.gov/nvlap>.

1.6.2   NIST Handbook 150 Checklist

All NVLAP programs use the NIST Handbook 150 Checklist, which contains the requirements published in NIST Handbook 150. The checklist items are numbered to correspond to clauses 4 and 5 and annexes A and B of NIST Handbook 150. The current version of the checklist is available from the NVLAP website at <http://www.nist.gov/nvlap>.

1.6.3   NIST Handbook 150-17 Checklist

1.6.3.1 The NIST Handbook 150-17 Checklist (also referred to as the CST Program-Specific Checklist) addresses the requirements specific to cryptographic and security testing given in NIST Handbook 150-17. The checklist contains the requirements provided in this handbook, including testing requirements and additional details and notes for the assessor(s) (e.g., the names of the key personnel), with an emphasis on observing and performing tests, testing accuracy, instrumentation, calibration, personnel competency, and test reporting. The current version of the checklist is available from the CST LAP website at <http://www.nist.gov/pml/nvlap/nvlap-cst-lap.cfm>.

1.6.3.2 The CST Program-Specific Checklist applies only to cryptographic and security testing. The checklist focuses on the testing requirements and the special personnel and equipment requirements corresponding to the types of tests elected by the applicant laboratory. Annexes A through E provide additional information and requirements on the types of tests and their derived requirements.

1.6.3.3 The checklist concludes with a Comments and Nonconformities section used by the assessor(s) to explicitly identify and describe all nonconformities noted in the body of the checklist. Additionally, the assessor(s) may use the form to document comments on any aspect of the laboratory or its performance.

1.6.4   Scope of accreditation and test method selection

1.6.4.1 The CST LAP offers a set of test methods for accreditation. Depending on the breadth of its testing capabilities, the applicant laboratory may select test(s) from the list of offered test methods. All the test methods for accreditation under this LAP have a prerequisite to meet the Basic Cryptographic and

Security (17BCS) test method. Some of the other test methods have additional prerequisites which are identified in the test-specific annex(es).

1.6.4.2 The scope of accreditation is determined by the test methods on the Test Method Selection List, which is provided to a laboratory seeking accreditation as part of the NVLAP application package for the program. For additional information regarding the methods available for selection, refer to Annex A of this handbook.

1.6.5 CST Template for Oral Quizzing

The assessor(s) use(s) the CST Template for Oral Quizzing as a means to document the information gathered during the oral quizzing conducted during the on-site assessment. The template captures the questions asked, the personnel participating in the quiz and any assessor(s) comments regarding the responses provided by the laboratory personnel.

1.6.6 NVLAP Lab Bulletins

NVLAP Lab Bulletins are issued to laboratories and assessors, when needed, to clarify program-specific requirements and to provide information about the most current program additions and changes. Lab Bulletins providing additions or changes to the current program will supersede the requirements of the current published handbook until such time as the additions or changes are published in a revision of the handbook.

1.6.7 Other publications

Some of the tests and associated test methods reference additional documentation that can be found in the annex associated with the specific test methods and/or on the CST LAP website. The types of tests are available on the NVLAP website at <http://www.nist.gov/pml/nvlap/nvlap-cst-lap.cfm>.

2 LAP establishment, development and implementation

2.1 Basis for establishment

There are no requirements additional to those set forth in NIST Handbook 150.

2.2 Development of technical requirements

All technical requirements mandated for a laboratory under accreditation tailor the requirements discussed in clauses 4 and 5, which are derived from the elected scope of accreditation and associated test methods for which a candidate requests accreditation.

2.3 Announcing the establishment of a LAP

There are no requirements additional to those set forth in NIST Handbook 150.

2.4   Adding to or modifying a LAP

Upon identifying the need for additional cryptographic and/or security tests or test types, NVLAP reserves the right to add or modify the CST LAP either by adding new subsidiary programs or new test methods to existing programs, or modifying the existing test methods. All changes will be published in a timely manner in a NVLAP Lab Bulletin and will be reflected on the NVLAP website: <http://www.nist.gov/nvlap>.

2.5   Termination of a LAP

There are no requirements additional to those set forth in NIST Handbook 150.

3   Accreditation process

3.1   Application for accreditation

3.1.1   A laboratory interested in accreditation for any of the types of tests offered under the CST LAP shall review and become familiar with all the requirements listed in NIST Handbook 150 and in this handbook, review the CST LAP website at <http://www.nist.gov/pml/nvlap/nvlap-cst-lap.cfm>, and contact NVLAP for the most current updates on the requirements and application process.

3.1.2   The accreditation process starts with the submission of the laboratory's application and fees payment. Once the application is deemed complete, the process continues with the on-site assessment visit and the laboratory's proficiency testing evaluation, which includes the a) through d) steps represented below. Upon completion of any corrective action response(s) to any nonconformities found during the on-site assessment visit and/or proficiency testing evaluation, the process ends with NVLAP's final decision regarding the laboratory's accreditation.

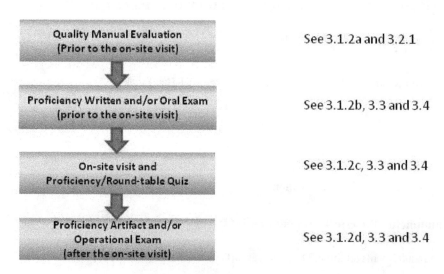

Figure 2. Accreditation flowchart.

a) **Quality manual evaluation** – When the laboratory is applying for accreditation, the assessor(s) must first determine that the management system meets the requirements.

b) **Proficiency written and/or oral exam** – For initial accreditation, once the assessor(s) determines that the management system meets the requirements, a written exam may then be provided to the applicant laboratory depending upon the intended scope, with a seven-calendar-day deadline for response, unless otherwise specified. This exam evaluates the laboratory personnel's technical expertise and knowledge of the standards and test methods applicable to the scope of accreditation for which the laboratory is applying. The laboratory shall score greater than 75 % correct responses for the accreditation process to continue and the on-site visit to be scheduled. For some test methods (e.g., NPIVP and SCAP), an oral exam is necessary to demonstrate proficiency regarding specific tests. The technical expert(s) from the associated technical program conducts this exam via a teleconference with the laboratory personnel. The oral exam is normally scheduled two weeks prior to the scheduled on-site assessment visit.

c) **On-site visit and proficiency/round-table quiz** – If applicable, once the written exam is passed for an applicant in its initial accreditation process, an on-site visit is scheduled at a mutually agreed-upon date and time. For all applicants, the on-site assessment visit is scheduled once it is determined that the management system meets or continues to meet the necessary requirements found in NIST Handbook 150 and NIST Handbook 150-17. During the on-site visit, the laboratory's personnel will be quizzed and team dynamics observed for proficiency and expertise in the technical area for which the laboratory is applying for accreditation. Staff member interaction and knowledge distribution among team members are key factors that will be monitored by the assessor(s). The laboratory staff shall provide greater than 75 % correct responses for the accreditation process to continue. The laboratory must also demonstrate during the on-site visit that the required set of tools is available and the testing environment is adequate (e.g., space, ventilation, security, test chambers, and test benches) for the test methods for which accreditation is sought.

d) **Proficiency artifact and/or operational exam** – Once the assessor(s) determines that the laboratory has satisfactorily completed the on-site visit, a proficiency artifact and/or operational exam is provided to the applicant laboratory (at the end of the initial on-site visit or after on-site visit). Unless otherwise specified by NVLAP, the laboratory shall complete the test by the scope-dependent deadline. The proficiency artifact and/or operational exam is designed to evaluate the laboratory's understanding of and competence to apply the Cryptographic and Security Testing conformance testing methodology specific to the scope of accreditation for which the laboratory is applying. The laboratory shall successfully complete the proficiency test and/or operational exam as evaluated by the technical expert assessor(s).

3.2 Activities prior to initial on-site assessment

3.2.1 The quality manual and related documentation shall contain or refer to documentation that describes and details the implementation of procedures covering all of the technical requirements in this handbook. This information will be reviewed by a NVLAP assessor(s) prior to the on-site assessment. If the quality manual is judged unsatisfactory, the on-site visit will be postponed. Otherwise, nonconformities and recommendations for management system enhancements will be discussed during the on-site visit.

3.2.2 For some of the test methods, the test tools are available for download upon request from NVLAP and/or registration with the validation authority to obtain the credentials to download and decrypt the tools. Other methods require the assessor(s) to determine whether the laboratory is ready to be trained to use the test tools before receiving them at its initial on-site evaluation. In other cases, the test tools will be provided to the laboratory during the on-site visit or provided to the laboratory after accreditation has been granted. When available, the laboratory shall register, download and install the test tool before the NVLAP assessor(s) arrive(s). The laboratory will be responsible for demonstrating, if required, competence to prepare and use these tools. This demonstration will include: loading, configuring and running the tools; preparing the test reports; and performing updates if necessary. A complete test report produced by the laboratory using these tools should be available for discussion as instructed, either during or after the on-site visit. Distribution and confidentiality of test tools may have specific validation authority restrictions.

3.3 On-site assessments

3.3.1 Conduct of on-site assessment

3.3.1.1 It is important to note that the laboratory cannot be granted accreditation unless:

a) the laboratory has completed and passed the written exam and/or oral exam (NPIVP, SCAP) [3.1.2b] (normally conducted before the initial on-site assessment);

b) the laboratory has passed the proficiency quiz [3.1.2c] (normally conducted during the on-site assessment);

c) the laboratory has completed and passed the proficiency artifact test and/or operational exam [3.1.2d];

d) the laboratory staff has demonstrated an understanding of and competence to apply the Cryptographic and Security Testing conformance testing methodology as evaluated by the results of the proficiency test;

e) the laboratory has exercised the management system and has produced appropriate records of all management system activities; and

f) the laboratory has demonstrated for the selected test(s) that the required set of tools and test methods are available and the testing environment is adequate (e.g., space, ventilation, security, separation, storage, test chambers and test benches) .

3.3.1.2 The time span for the on-site assessment is dependent upon the applicant's scope of accreditation. Typically, the on-site assessment will span about two to three days and will be performed by two or more NVLAP assessors. All observations made by the assessor(s) during the assessment are held in the strictest confidence.

3.3.1.3 In some cases, the on-site assessment may involve the laboratory site and a separate test site for the proficiency testing. If the separate test site for the proficiency demonstration is within a short commuting distance from the main laboratory site, the demonstration will have to be scheduled at a date and time mutually agreed-upon between the assessor(s) and laboratory management, but will still be part of the on-site visit. If the geographic distance to the separate test site requires significant travel, then this is deemed by NVLAP to be a separate laboratory that will have to be separately accredited with its own separate on-site assessment.

3.3.1.4 The assessor(s) will use, in addition to the general checklist based on NIST Handbook 150, the CST Program-Specific Checklist derived from the technical specifics contained in this handbook. Even though the CST checklist is derived dynamically from the elected scope of accreditation and corresponding test methods, the derivation is done such that the composed checklist ensures that the assessment is complete and that each assessor covers the same items at laboratories with an equivalent chosen scope of accreditation.

3.3.1.5 Additionally, the assigned assessor(s) has the right and the responsibility to go beyond the checklist whenever the need arises (e.g., new updated requirement are available on the CST LAP's website but are not incorporated yet in the checklist), in order to delve more deeply into technical issues.

NOTE   NVLAP will document all technical requirements prior to assessments.

3.3.1.6 The agenda for a typical on-site assessment is given below.

a) **Opening meeting:** During the on-site visit, the assessor(s) conduct(s) an entry briefing with laboratory management and supervisory personnel to explain the purpose of the on-site and to discuss the schedule for the assessment activities.   Information provided by the laboratory on the accreditation application form may be discussed during this meeting. At the discretion of the laboratory manager, other staff may attend this meeting.

b) **Staff interviews, discussions, proficiency quizzes:** The assessor will ask the laboratory manager to assist in arranging times for individual interviews with laboratory staff members and/or proficiency/round-table quizzes of staff. While it is not necessary for the assessor to talk to all staff members if individual interviews are requested, he/she may select staff members representing all different aspects of the laboratory. If proficiency/round-table quizzes are to be conducted on-site, all members of the relevant staff shall be scheduled to be present and participate. Also, if after the completion of the round-table quizzing of the laboratory staff it is deemed necessary by the assessor(s), further interviews with individual laboratory staff members may be requested.

c) **Records review:** During the on-site visit, the assessor(s) will also review the laboratory's documentation, including:

- conformance of the quality system with ISO/IEC 17025:2005 and NIST Handbook 150;
- quality manual;
- equipment and maintenance records;
- record-keeping procedures;
- testing procedures;
- laboratory test reports;
- personnel competency records;
- personnel training records including, but not limited to, training plans, areas of training, and training materials;
- version of the test tools and/or other test program-specific software;
- procedures for updating pertinent information; and
- safeguards and separation for the protection of confidential, vendor-sensitive, proprietary and applicable International Traffic in Arms Regulations (ITAR) information.

One (or more) laboratory staff member(s) shall be available to answer questions; however, the assessor may wish to review the documents alone. Under some circumstances, the assessor may remove some documents from the laboratory during the assessment. Specifically, the assessor may remove for review documents related to the quality system, such as a revised quality manual, proficiency test data, or new procedures. The material will be returned or destroyed at the laboratory's direction.

The assessor will check personnel information for job descriptions, resumes, training records and technical performance reviews. The assessor shall not be given information which violates individual privacy such as salary, medical information, or performance reviews outside the scope of the laboratory's accreditation. At the discretion of the laboratory, a member of its human resources department (or equivalent) may be present during the review of personnel information.

d) **Internal audit and management review:** The assessor(s) will review and discuss the laboratory's internal audit and management review activities with the laboratory staff. The discussion will include all aspects of those activities including the management system procedures, the audit findings, the results of the management review, and the actions taken to resolve problems identified.

e) **Equipment:** The assessor(s) will examine test method-specific computer hardware, software, supporting test equipment, and facilities for appropriateness, capability, adherence to specifications, etc.

f) **Laboratory walk-through:** The assessor(s) will inspect the laboratory in the following areas during a walk-through:

- physical layout of the laboratory including entrance and exit points;

- all test equipment and tools, including computer hardware, servers used for records retention and physical storage area;

- work environment in regard to providing adequate testing work space (including adequate separation of work activities as appropriate or by programmatic requirement), heating, lighting, etc.; and

- physical security including access control procedures and records.

g) **Proficiency evaluations:** Although the written examination is provided prior to the initial on-site assessment, the group round-table quizzes and individual demonstrations conducted during the initial and renewal on-site assessments are considered part of the proficiency evaluations. When necessary, there may be additional proficiency artifact and/or operational exams required as part of the assessment. Unless otherwise instructed prior to the on-site visit, the proficiency artifact and/or operational exam described in 3.1.2 and which completes the initial proficiency evaluations will be either provided at the end of the on-site visit or will be sent to the laboratory after the on-site visit. NVLAP reserves the right to modify this rule, when appropriate, on a case-by-case basis.

h) **Closing meeting:** At the end of the on-site visit, a closing meeting is held with the laboratory manager and staff to discuss any nonconformities documented by the assessor(s) during the visit. See 3.3.3.6 and 3.3.3.7 of NIST Handbook 150 for more information regarding the assessment report, nonconformities and the final resolution.

3.3.2   On-site assessment report

The assessor completes the On-Site Assessment Report that summarizes the findings. Copies of the completed checklists are also attached to the report at the closing meeting. The report is signed by the assessor(s) and the laboratory's Authorized Representative.   The original report and checklists are forwarded to NVLAP as required by NIST Handbook 150, 3.3.2.3.   A copy of the report and of the checklists is given to the laboratory representative for retention. The decision to grant or renew accreditation is not made by the assessor team but is made by NVLAP in accordance with the procedures described in NIST Handbook 150.

3.3.3 Nonconformities, comments, and recommendations

3.3.3.1 A nonconformity that has been corrected during the on-site assessment by the laboratory using its corrective action process and any recommendations will be specifically noted on the on-site assessment report by the assessor. The assessor will also note how the nonconformity was resolved.

3.3.3.2 Comments in the report should be given serious consideration by the laboratory, but no action is mandated and changes are made at the laboratory's discretion. Comments are those areas of concern where a nonconformity may arise; however, no objective evidence is available to support citing a nonconformity. Historically, it has been noted that comments often rise to the level of nonconformities on subsequent assessments. As such, comments noted in the assessment will be reviewed at the next on-site assessment to ensure that these issues have not risen to the level of nonconformities since the last on-site visit.

3.3.3.3 Positive feedback will also be recorded on the on-site assessment report.

3.4 Proficiency Testing

3.4.1 General

3.4.1.1 The CST LAP mandates program-specific proficiency testing. All applicant laboratories are required to participate in proficiency testing for all test methods derived from their scope of accreditation, as designated in the annex associated with the specific test methods.

3.4.1.2 The proficiency test concept is designed to allow the evaluation of the laboratory's ability to produce repeatable and reproducible test data. To properly evaluate a laboratory, the proficiency testing consists of several parts previously described in 3.1.2.

3.4.2 Types of proficiency testing

NVLAP follows ISO/IEC 17043 for the types of proficiency testing used within the CST LAP, therefore, the LAP's proficiency testing may consist of one or more of the following exercises:

a) Demonstration of correct identification and use of the NVLAP/NIST-mandated test tools. The laboratory shall demonstrate that all appropriate personnel, including those performing testing, understand the test tools and/or component use and operation. This shall be demonstrated by the laboratory personnel exercising the use of the publicly-available or provided test tools under the assessor(s)' direct observation.

b) Demonstration of an understanding and correct interpretation of all data transformation and of all test results reported by the test tools.

c) Demonstration of report generation in an approved format and with the content identical to the results produced by the test tools.

d) Demonstration of a solid background, theoretical knowledge and technical expertise in the area of the elected test methods for the scope of accreditation. The laboratory shall be provided with a proficiency quiz to be responded to by all appropriate personnel including those performing testing. The quiz also poses questions for each test method for which the laboratory is seeking accreditation.

These questions will test for:

- basic cryptographic and security knowledge as applicable to the technical area determined by the elected test methods on the scope of accreditation;

- familiarity with the governing standards and specifications;

- familiarity with the test methods derived from the elected test methods on the scope of accreditation;

- ability to determine how a particular cryptographic or security test should be performed for a particular set of test requirements; and

- how a specific algorithm, module or component should be tested to the governing specification.

e) Demonstration of IUT or SUT conformance testing proficiency. The laboratory shall perform a conformance test of a specially designed artifact, referred to as IUT or SUT, with one or more features that is/are not in conformance with the standard. The laboratory shall discover the nonconformities, document them, and indicate which standard's requirements have failed due to the presence of the nonconformities.

Unless otherwise specified by NVLAP, the proficiency artifact and/or operational exam for the initial accreditation will be delivered to the laboratory at the end of the on-site assessment or later. Also, unless otherwise stated, the proficiency artifact shall be considered the property of the programmatic body and shall be considered confidential property not to be shared, divulged, or changed without permission from the associated programmatic body. Any use of the artifact outside of the specified task may result in adverse action regarding the laboratory's accreditation.

NVLAP, in collaboration with all CST validation programs, considers the validation reports submitted to the validation programs as ongoing proficiency tests.

3.4.3 Analysis and reporting

The results of the proficiency testing are presented by the assessor(s) and/or the validation program to NVLAP as soon as the testing process is completed. The results are then reported to the candidate laboratory within 30 days from the completion of the testing process.

3.4.4 Proficiency testing nonconformities

Problems resulting from the results of any proficiency testing will be discussed with appropriate laboratory personnel responsible for developing and implementing plans for resolving the problems. For nonconformities identified by proficiency testing during an on-site assessment, a scheduled proficiency testing, or submission of a test report for validation of a vendor's product shall be resolved by the laboratory in order to attain and/or maintain accreditation.

A large number of errors in the reports submitted to any of the validation programs can trigger the suspension or revocation of a laboratory's accreditation. For more information, see 3.10.

3.5 Accreditation decision

There are no requirements additional to those set forth in NIST Handbook 150.

3.6 Granting accreditation

It is important to note that the laboratory cannot be granted initial accreditation unless the laboratory has effectively implemented the management system and has produced appropriate records of all management system activities, including conducting at least one internal audit and one management review.

3.7 Renewal of accreditation

There are no requirements additional to those set forth in NIST Handbook 150.

3.8 Monitoring visits

There are no requirements additional to those set forth in NIST Handbook 150.

3.9 Changes to scope of accreditation

There are no requirements additional to those set forth in NIST Handbook 150.

3.10 Suspension of accreditation

3.10.1 Failure to appropriately address and resolve complaints from customers or other interested parties may result in a NVLAP surveillance activity, additional proficiency testing, and/or suspension or revocation of accreditation.

3.10.2 Significant changes in a laboratory's key technical personnel or facilities may result in a NVLAP monitoring visit(s), and/or suspension of accreditation of the affected test method(s) from the scope of accreditation if the new personnel prove inadequately prepared or unsuited for the job or the facilities are inadequate to support the testing. Loss of key personnel without immediate adequate replacement may result in suspension of the laboratory's accreditation for the test method(s) affected by the lost of key personnel.

3.10.3 If the laboratory does not demonstrate continued competence to perform CST conformance testing and validations, NVLAP may suspend or revoke the laboratory's accreditation. The accreditation may be suspended or revoked if, any of the following statements is true:

- 25 % or more of the reports submitted for validation within one year are incorrect, invalid or deficient as defined by each validation program;
- more than 60 % of the personnel that participated in the latest (re)accreditation process have left the laboratory;
- nonconformities are found during any on-site visit and are not addressed through corrective actions taken by the laboratory: or

- the laboratory has not submitted any vendor product test report to the validation body in the last two years.

All issues surrounding the need to suspend and/or revoke a laboratory's accreditation are reviewed on a case-by-case basis.

3.11 Denial and revocation of accreditation

There are no requirements additional to those set forth in NIST Handbook 150.

3.12 Voluntary termination of accreditation

There are no requirements additional to those set forth in NIST Handbook 150.

3.13 Appeals

There are no requirements additional to those set forth in NIST Handbook 150.

4 Management requirements for accreditation

4.1 Organization

4.1.1 The laboratory shall establish and maintain policies and procedures for maintaining laboratory impartiality and integrity in the conduct of cryptographic and security testing. To avoid any conflict of interest, the laboratory policies and procedures shall ensure that neither the applicant laboratory nor other divisions within its parent corporation can perform conformance testing if is currently providing or has previously provided consulting services to the vendor for the IUT or SUT (e.g., develop testing evidence, design advice).

NOTE A CST laboratory may perform consulting services to provide clarification of the standards, the Derived Test Requirements, and other associated documents at any time during the life cycle of the IUT or SUT.

4.1.2 For any other services of the laboratory's parent corporation not listed in 4.1.1, the laboratory shall have an explicit policy and a set of procedures for maintaining a strict separation, both physical and electronic, between the laboratory testers and company's consultant teams, product developers, system integrators, and others who may have an interest in and/or may unduly influence the testing outcome.

4.1.3 A CST laboratory shall have no financial interest for the work performed under the present scope of accreditation other than its conformance testing and/or validation fees.

4.1.4 The laboratory shall not perform conformance testing on a module for which the laboratory has:

a) designed any part of the IUT or SUT;

b) developed original documentation for any part of the IUT or SUT;

c) built, coded or implemented any part of the IUT or SUT; or

d) had any ownership or vested interest in the IUT or SUT.

NOTE   Provided that a CST laboratory has met the other requirements, the laboratory may perform conformance testing on IUT or SUT produced by a company when:

- the laboratory has no ownership in the company;
- the laboratory has a completely separate management from the company; and
- business between the CST laboratory and the company is performed under contractual agreements, as done with other clients.

4.1.5   A CST laboratory may take existing vendor documentation for an IUT or SUT (post-design and post-development) and consolidate or reformat the information (from multiple sources) into a set format. If this occurs, the validation programs shall be notified of this when the conformance test report is submitted.

4.1.6   For additional guidance on laboratory organization, additional interpretations and clarifications concerning the conflict of interest and strategies for avoiding it, consult also the guidance provided by each validation program. If any discrepancy in the provided information regarding accreditation process and/or conflict of interest arises, NVLAP's guidance supersedes any other program-specific documentation.

4.2   Management system

4.2.1   The management system shall include policies and procedures to ensure the protection of proprietary information. The policies and procedures shall specify how proprietary information will be protected from persons outside the laboratory, from visitors to the laboratory, from laboratory personnel without a need to know, and from other unauthorized persons.

4.2.2   The laboratory shall comply with all policies and procedures to ensure technical integrity of the conformance testing analyses and results.

4.2.3   The reference documents listed in 1.4, the annex associated with the specific test methods, and the program's website, as well as any other standards and publications related to the CST LAP, shall be available to all appropriate personnel at all times.

4.3   Document control

There are no requirements additional to those set forth in NIST Handbook 150.

4.4   Review of requests, tenders and contracts

4.4.1   If the laboratory conducts testing at any selected site other than the laboratory's site accredited for conformance testing, the site shall meet all requirements pertinent to the conformance testing of the IUT or SUT as the accredited testing laboratory.

NOTE   The laboratory may use checklists and/or contract agreements to satisfy this requirement.

4.4.2   Policies for documents storage and maintenance of contracts under confidentiality, nondisclosure agreements, marked as secret, or copyright protected, shall be well defined according to the document's status. These documents shall be protected commensurate with their classification and/or sensitivity, and access to them shall be given only to authorized personnel.

4.4.3   The testing laboratory and vendor shall agree, in writing, what constitutes the IUT or SUT and what constitutes the environment within the IUT. For this program, the environment includes, but it is not limited to:

a)   the specific test platform;

b)   the test configuration; and

c)   the external environment.

4.5   Subcontracting of tests and calibrations

If subcontracting is used as a mechanism by which the laboratory fulfills and/or enhances the conformance testing process, the subcontracting laboratory shall employ either services provided only by NVLAP-accredited laboratories whose scope includes the applicable test method(s) or by laboratories that satisfy all testing requirements as indicated in NIST Handbook 150, NIST Handbook 150-17 and all documents pertaining to the validation program. In the latter instance, the subcontracting laboratory:

a)   shall justify the selection explaining why this particular subcontractor was selected and how the subcontractor satisfies the testing requirements; and

b)   shall assume full responsibility for the outcome of the conformance testing performed by the subcontractor.

4.6   Purchasing services and supplies

There are no requirements additional to those set forth in NIST Handbook 150.

4.7   Service to the customer

There are no requirements additional to those set forth in NIST Handbook 150.

4.8   Complaints

There are no requirements additional to those set forth in NIST Handbook 150.

4.9   Control of nonconforming testing and/or calibration work

There are no requirements additional to those set forth in NIST Handbook 150.

4.10   Improvement

There are no requirements additional to those set forth in NIST Handbook 150.

4.11   Corrective action

There are no requirements additional to those set forth in NIST Handbook 150.

4.12   Preventive action

There are no requirements additional to those set forth in NIST Handbook 150.

4.13   Control of records

4.13.1   General

4.13.1.1 The laboratory shall maintain a functional record-keeping system for each customer. Records shall be readily accessible and complete. Digital media shall be logged and properly marked, and they shall be properly and securely backed-up. Entries in paper-based laboratory notebooks shall be dated and signed or initialed.

4.13.1.2 Software and data protected by nondisclosure agreements or classified as confidential shall be stored according to the vendor and/or government requirements and commensurate with the data sensitivity, and access shall be granted only to the authorized personnel. An access log file shall be maintained.

4.13.1.3 If a vendor's system on which testing is conducted is potentially open to access by third parties, the testing laboratory shall ensure that the testing environment is controlled so that the third parties do not gain access to that system during testing.

4.13.1.4 Records of all management system activities including training, internal audits, and management reviews shall be securely saved for future reviews. The integrity of electronic documents shall be assured by means commensurate with the data sensitivity. Documents in hard copy form shall be marked and stored in a secure location and, if necessary, a file logging any access, change, or addition shall be maintained to preserve a document's integrity and prevent unauthorized changes.

4.13.1.5 Laboratories shall maintain records of the configuration of test equipment and all analyses to ensure the suitability of test equipment to perform the desired testing.

4.13.2   Technical records

4.13.2.1 The final test results and/or the test reports generated using cryptographic or security testing tools for the IUT or SUT shall be kept by the laboratory following the completion of testing for the life of the IUT or SUT, or as specified by the validation body and/or vendor in writing. Records may include hard or digital copies of the official test results and the test results error file(s). Records shall be stored in a manner that assures survivability, confidentiality, integrity, and accessibility.

4.13.2.2 A copy of the final test results and/or the test reports generated using cryptographic or security testing tools for the IUT shall be submitted to the validation program.

4.14 Internal audits

In the case where only one member of a laboratory staff is competent in some technical aspects of the program, or is the only expert in conducting a specific aspect of the conformance testing, an external audit by an appropriate expert shall be necessary in order to audit this technical aspect. An audit shall include, at a minimum, but not be limited to:

a) a review of documentation and instructions;

b) adherence to procedures and instructions; and

c) documentation of the audit findings.

4.15 Management reviews

The laboratory shall perform at least one full management review prior to the first on-site assessment.

5 Technical requirements for accreditation

5.1 General

The quality manual shall contain, or refer to documentation that describes and details the laboratory's implementation of procedures covering all of the technical requirements in NIST Handbook 150 and this handbook.

5.2 Personnel

5.2.1 Within each laboratory's elected scope of accreditation, the laboratory shall maintain responsible supervisory personnel and competent technical staff that are:

a) knowledgeable of all relevant FIPS, NIST Special Publications (SP), and references in this handbook and on the CST LAP website;

b) familiar with cryptographic terminology and families of cryptographic algorithms and security functions with particular emphasis on the FIPS-approved and/or NIST-recommended security functions;

c) familiar with the cryptographic and security testing tools; and

d) knowledgeable of all programmatic test methods, test metrics, and implementation guidance.

5.2.2 The laboratory shall maintain a list of the key personnel designated to satisfy NVLAP requirements, including their assigned roles and a brief summary of their latest training qualifications. The list shall include, but shall not be limited to:

a) Laboratory's Director;

b) Laboratory Manager;

c) Quality Manager;

d) Authorized Representative;

e) Approved Signatories; and

f) Other key technical persons in the laboratory (e.g., testers).

NOTE Significant changes in a laboratory's key technical personnel or facilities may result in a NVLAP monitoring visit(s), and/or suspension of accreditation if the new personnel prove inadequately prepared or unsuited for the job(s). Loss of key personnel without immediate adequate replacement may result in the laboratory's suspension.

5.2.3 If the mechanism by which the laboratory employs staff members is through contracting of personnel, any key personnel who are contractors shall be identified and listed in the laboratory's application for accreditation. When a change in the key personnel employed through subcontracting occurs or when the direct supervision of this category of personnel is not possible, a report shall be submitted to NVLAP and to the affected validation program.

NOTE Any of the above-listed changes in the personnel employed through subcontracting can affect laboratory's accreditation status.

5.2.4 An individual may be assigned or appointed to serve in more than one position; however, to the extent possible, the laboratory director and the quality manager positions should be independently staffed.

5.2.5 The quality manager shall receive management system training preferably in ISO/IEC 17025. If training is not available in ISO/IEC 17025, minimum training shall be acquired in the ISO 9000 series, especially ISO 9001, or equivalent with particular emphasis on internal auditor training.

5.2.6 The laboratory shall have staff members with knowledge and skills commensurate with the scope of work such as a technical degree (e.g. a Bachelor degree in Computer Science, Computer Engineering, Electrical Engineering, etc.), similar technical discipline or equivalent experience (e.g. professional certification, etc.). For more details regarding the staff members' required expertise for each program, see the annex associated with the specific test methods.

5.2.7 The laboratory shall ensure adequate training for the laboratory staff as directed in this subclause and in the associated annex, for the specific training requirements derived from the laboratory's scope(s) of accreditation. The personnel shall possess knowledge of, or be trained prior to accreditation on/in the areas listed below:

a) general requirements of the test methods, including generation of test reports;

b) system security concepts;

c) physical security;

d) identification and authentication technologies and techniques;

e) familiarity with cryptographic and security terminology;

f) standards compliance;

g) familiarity with all FIPS publications referenced in this document and NIST Handbook 150;

h) operation and maintenance of NVLAP/Validation Program-mandated testing tools; and

i) familiarity with the Internet and Internet-related software and the ability to locate and securely download references and information from a given website.

5.2.8 The laboratory shall have a competency review program and procedures for the evaluation and maintenance of the competency of each staff member for each test method the staff member is authorized to conduct. An evaluation and an observation of performance shall be conducted annually for each staff member by the immediate supervisor or a designee appointed by the laboratory director. A record of the annual evaluation of each staff member shall be dated and signed by the supervisor and the employee.

5.2.9 If more than 60 % of the personnel that participated in the latest (re)accreditation process has left the laboratory, the laboratory shall inform NVLAP. NVLAP will assign a nonconformity to the laboratory due to the inability to demonstrate competence. The laboratory shall address the nonconformity through corrective and preventive actions. NVLAP reserves the right to require a reassessment if considered necessary.

5.2.10 For scope of accreditation and test method-specific requirements additional to those set forth in 5.2, see the annex associated with the specific test methods.

5.3   Accommodation and environmental conditions

5.3.1 The laboratory shall have its internal networks protected from unauthorized access by external entities, as well as protection against malicious software, worms, viruses, spybots, etc.

5.3.2 If the laboratory is conducting multiple simultaneous testing activities, a system of separation between IUTs and SUTs of different vendors and conformance testing activities shall be maintained as necessary.

5.3.3 The laboratory shall have Internet access for obtaining the most current documentation and test tools from NIST/ITL or NVLAP or other appropriate sites and secure e-mail capabilities for communication with NVLAP, NIST/ITL, CSEC, and the laboratory's customers.

5.3.4 The testing laboratory shall ensure that, when applicable, the correct version of the NIST/ITL-or NVLAP-provided testing tools are used and that the tools have not been altered in any way that might lead to incorrect results.

5.3.5 For all conformance testing and validations, the laboratory shall ensure that any file containing old results or old test programs on the IUT or SUT is isolated from the current test programs and test or validation results.

5.3.6 If a laboratory must conduct conformance testing at a location outside the laboratory facility, the environment shall conform, as appropriate, to the requirements for the laboratory site, and shall be checked by the NVLAP-accredited laboratory as a responsible party for the security of the environment and the integrity of all tests and recorded results.

For additional information see 4.4.3.

5.3.7 For test method-specific requirements additional to those set forth in 5.3, see the annex associated with the specific test methods.

5.4 Test and calibration methods and method validation

5.4.1 General

Tests may be conducted at the vendor or laboratory site or at another mutually agreed-upon site. When testing is performed at a vendor site, all NVLAP requirements pertaining to equipment and environment as they apply to the tests scheduled outside the laboratory's accredited location, shall apply. Moreover, only the personnel of the NVLAP-accredited laboratory shall perform all actions necessary to conduct the tests and record the results, including the loading, compiling, configuring, and execution of any of the mandated testing tools.

5.4.2 Selection of methods

For more specific information regarding test methods selection, see the annex associated with the specific test methods.

5.5 Equipment

5.5.1 For its scope of accreditation, the laboratory shall have appropriate hardware, software, test tools and computer facilities to conduct cryptographic and security testing. This includes, but is not limited to:

a) required software test suites;

b) testing equipment for physical tests; and

c) all special equipment necessary to perform all tests derived from the most current version of the standard.

5.5.2 Special equipment may be necessary for particular test methods as derived from the scope of accreditation. For more information regarding types of equipment and information required for conducting the conformance tests, see the annex associated with the specific test method(s).

5.5.3 The equipment used for conducting cryptographic and security testing shall be maintained in accordance with the manufacturer's recommendations and in accordance with internally documented laboratory procedures, as applicable. Test equipment refers to software and hardware products and/or other assessment mechanisms used by the laboratory to support the cryptographic and security testing of the IUT or SUT.

5.5.4 A list of the required testing tools for each test is provided in the annex associated with the specific test method(s) and/or the CST LAP website. For conformance testing, the laboratory shall own, load and run a copy of the testing tool(s) provided by the validation program and produce test results using the tool(s) as appropriate. The testing tools provided by the validation program shall not be altered or changed and shall not be distributed outside the laboratory except to the validation program.

5.5.5 Whenever major or minor changes are made to any testing tool, a testing laboratory shall have procedures to assure the accurate execution and correct performance of the test tool. The procedures shall include, at a minimum, the complete set of regression testing of the test tool. This is necessary to ensure that consistency is maintained, as appropriate, with other testing laboratories and that correctness is maintained with respect to the relevant standard(s) or specification(s).

5.5.6 For a given test tool, there may be no suitable validation service available outside the testing laboratory to which accreditation is applicable, and no suitable reference implementation that could be used by the testing laboratory to validate the test tool. In this situation, the testing laboratory shall define and document the procedures and methods that it uses to check on the correct operation of the test tool, and provide evidence that these procedures and methods are applied whenever the test tool is modified.

5.5.7 The testing laboratory shall document and follow appropriate procedures whenever a test tool is suspected or found to contain errors that make the tool defective or unfit for use. These procedures shall include establishing that there is a genuine error, reporting the error to the appropriate maintenance authority or validation body. If the conformance testing results change for an IUT or SUT after correcting the test tool then the information shall be transmitted to the vendor and validation authority.

5.5.8 The calibration of the hardware and software shall be accomplished through:

a) configuration management for all hardware and software; or

b) a version control system.

5.5.9 Records shall be kept of the date, extent of all hardware and software upgrades and updates and periods of use.

5.5.10 For test method-specific requirements additional to those set forth in 5.5, see the annex associated with the specific test method(s).

5.6   Measurement traceability

5.6.1   General

5.6.1.1 For cryptographic and security testing, "traceability" [see 1.5.37] is interpreted to mean that the validation test tools shall be traceable back to the underlying requirements of the normative standards listed in 1.4, in the annex associated with the specific test methods, and on the CST LAP website. This means that each abstract test case and the associated evaluation methodology are traceable to a specific cryptographic or security requirement listed in the governing documentary standard, and that the abstract tests cases are achieved via the assertions and associated DTRs documented in the testing tool in use. Test results produced by the testing laboratory shall be traceable to standard test suites when appropriate, or otherwise to the applicable authoritative test suite.

5.6.1.2 For test method specific requirements additional to those set forth in 5.6, see the annex associated with the specific test method(s).

5.6.2 Calibration

5.6.2.1 Test tools

5.6.2.1.1 The laboratory shall ensure that any test tool used to conduct cryptographic and security testing is performing properly according to the validation body specifications. The laboratory shall also examine to ensure that the tool does not interfere with the conduct of the test and does not modify or impact the IUT or SUT.

5.6.2.1.2 Confirmation of the use of the most current version of testing tools shall be assured before conducting a test. Records of these confirmations shall be maintained.

5.6.2.2 Test equipment

5.6.2.2.1 Laboratories shall maintain records of the configuration of test equipment and all analyses to ensure the suitability of test equipment to perform the desired testing.

5.6.2.2.2 If applicable, the equipment used for conducting the conformance tests shall be maintained and calibrated in accordance with the manufacturer's recommendation, as specified in the test method, or as specified in the annex associated with the specific test method(s).

5.6.2.2.3 For calibrations performed in-house, the reference standards used and the environmental conditions at the time of calibration shall be documented for all calibrations. Calibration records and evidence of the traceability of the reference standards used shall be made available for inspection during the on-site visit.

5.6.3 Testing

5.6.3.1 Laboratories shall use the test methods described in the annex associated with that specific method. When exceptions to the test methods are deemed necessary for technical reasons, the vendor and the validation program shall be informed and details shall be described in the test report. Documentation shall be provided on the test method exceptions taken to ensure that the correct and required precision and interpretation of the program-specific test method is maintained. When necessary, these reports may be used by the validation authority to update the test methods and the accompanying documentation.

The validation of a test method is the process of verifying as far as possible that the test method will produce results that are consistent with the specifications of the relevant program-specific requirements, with any relevant standards and, if applicable, with previously accepted, validated test methods (see 5.6.2.1).

5.6.3.2 In those technical areas where there is a difference between program-specific test objectives and the testing tool's abstract test cases, the testing laboratory shall show how each realization of a test case is derived faithfully from the governing FIPS, with preservation of assignment of verdicts or measurements to the corresponding sets of observations.

For more details on the specific test methods corresponding to the Cryptographic and Security Testing Accreditation program, see the annex associated with the specific test methods and the CST LAP website <http://www.nist.gov/pml/nvlap/nvlap-cst-lap.cfm>.

5.7   Sampling

There are no requirements additional to those set forth in NIST Handbook 150.

5.8   Handling of test and calibration items

5.8.1   Laboratories shall protect all IUTs, SUTs and test tools from modifications of any kind or unauthorized access and use.

5.8.2   When the IUT or SUT consists of software components, the laboratory shall ensure that a configuration management is in place to prevent inadvertent modifications. This configuration management shall uniquely identify each IUT or SUT and control and document modifications to any of the software components.

5.9   Assuring the quality of test and calibration results

There are no requirements additional to those set forth in NIST Handbook 150.

5.10   Reporting the results

5.10.1   General

The laboratory shall issue test reports of its work that accurately, clearly, and unambiguously present the test conditions, the test setup when it varies from the standard protocol, the test results, and all other information necessary to reproduce the test. Any deviations or omissions from the standard shall be clearly indicated. Test reports to customers shall meet contractual as well as programmatic requirements in addition to meeting the requirements of NIST Handbooks 150 and 150-17, governing FIPS and other standards. Test reports shall provide all necessary information to permit reproduction of the test and to obtain consistent results.

5.10.2   Test reports

5.10.2.1   If a validation program-supplied test report tool or other reporting methodologies are provided, the laboratory shall follow those requirements and use those supplied test tools.

5.10.2.2   If the testing laboratory includes comments, analyses or results in a test report that are not covered by the requirements of the governing FIPS, the laboratory shall state clearly which statements are outside the scope of its accreditation.

5.10.2.3   Whenever test cases are such that an analysis of the observations by the testing staff is required in order to interpret the results before stating them in a test report, the testing laboratory shall have objective procedures to be followed by the test operators performing the analysis, sufficient to ensure that the repeatability, reproducibility, and objectivity of the test results can be maintained.

5.10.2.4   Test reports bearing the NVLAP symbol may be written for more than one purpose:

a) *Reports that are produced under contract and intended for use by the vendor*

Reports intended for use only by the vendor shall meet vendor/laboratory contract obligations and be complete, but need not necessarily meet all validation program requirements.

b) *Reports to be submitted to Validation Authority for IUT or SUT validation under a specific validation program*

Test reports intended for submission to any of the validation programs under the CST LAP shall meet the requirements of the associated DTRs and the implementation guidance (IG) when applicable, as well as the requirements of NIST Handbook 150, NIST Handbook 150-17 and any other programmatic documentation guidance.

5.10.2.5 The laboratory shall perform an independent technical quality review of the test report submission documents prior to submission to the validation program. This shall address accuracy, completeness, sufficient evidence of test results and consistency. A record of this review shall be maintained.

5.10.3 Electronic transmission of results to the validation programs

5.10.3.1 A laboratory may submit either a printed or an electronic report as instructed by the validation program. The electronic version shall have the same content as the printed reports and shall be generated using a software application that is acceptable to the validation program.

5.10.3.2 The laboratory shall ensure that an integrity and confidentiality mechanism commensurable with the data sensitivity and/or programmatic requirements and/or government requirements when electronic delivery of the test reports to the validation program is employed to ensure that the test report cannot be disclosed to anyone other than the intended recipient(s) and an integrity mechanism exists to ensure that the test report is not modified.

5.10.4 Amendments to test reports and calibration certificates

5.10.4.1 For test reports created for validation purposes and submitted to any validation program under the CST LAP, the laboratory shall issue corrections or additions to a test report only by a supplementary document that is suitably marked and that meets the requirements of the respective validation program.

5.10.4.2 For test reports created for purposes other than official IUT validation, the laboratory shall issue corrections or additions to a test report only by a supplementary document suitably marked; e.g., "Supplement to test report serial number [...]". If the change involves a test assertion, this document shall specify which test assertion is in question, the content of the result, the explanation of the result, and the reason for acceptance of the result.

6   Additional requirements

See the following annexes for requirements specific to each technical program and its associated test methods.

Annex A
(informative)

Additional information about tests offered by the CST LAP

A.1 Additional general information

Annex A provides additional information as it pertains to the specific test methods for the various testing programs with the CST LAP. Section A.2 describes the various testing programs and the associated test methods available for accreditation under the CST LAP.

Figure A.1 is included to make a clear distinction between the accreditation program and the validation program, as well as to emphasize the separation of duties for each key player in these processes. This informative diagram illustrates the validation process and the rapport between:

- the validation authority (validation program, i.e., CAVP, CMVP, NPIVP, GSAP, SCAP);
- the third-party laboratory; and
- the consumers (e.g., U.S. Government agencies).

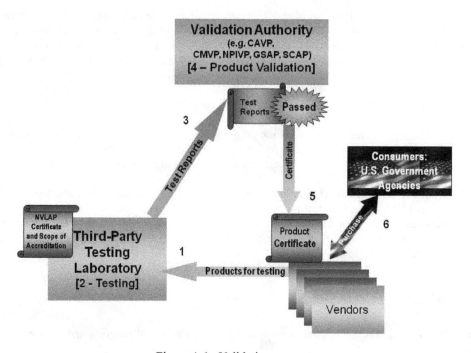

Figure A.1. Validation process.

A.2   Scope of accreditation and test methods

NVLAP offers all interested laboratories a flexible, dynamic system of selecting a compound scope of accreditation under the CST LAP that best fits the laboratory's level of expertise and equipment.

The minimum level of required expertise is described as "Basic Cryptographic and Security (17BCS)" testing and is considered the foundation of all test methods covered under the CST LAP. The Basic Cryptographic and Security (17BCS) testing scope is not a stand-alone scope and it is mandated as a prerequisite for all other test methods.   All other prerequisite information is found in the test specific annex.

A chained list showing all currently offered test methods is presented below. For the most current information on methods available, see the CST LAP website at:
<http://www.nist.gov/pml/nvlap/nvlap-cst-lap.cfm>.

The list below indicates that the election of any descendent test method mandates the election of all preceding test methods. For example, the selection of the 17CMH2 test, mandates the selection of the 17CMH1, 17CAV and 17BCS (included automatically) tests, as well.

☒   **17BCS** Basic Cryptographic and Security Testing (mandatory for all test methods)

    ☐   **17CAV** Cryptographic Algorithm Validation Testing (mandatory for 17CMH and 17CMS)

    ☐   **17CMH1** Cryptographic Hardware Modules – Hardware 1 Testing
        (FIPS 140-1 or successor, Security Levels 1 to 3)

        ☐   **17CMH2** Cryptographic Hardware Modules – Hardware 2 Testing
            (FIPS 140-1 or successor, Security Level 4)

    ☐   **17CMS1** Cryptographic Software Modules – Software 1 Testing
        (FIPS 140-1 or successor, Security Levels 1 to 3)

        ☐   **17CMS2** Cryptographic Software Modules – Software 2 Testing
            (FIPS 140-1 or successor, Security Level 4)

    ☐   **17PIV** Personal Identity Verification Testing (NPIVP, FIPS 201)

        ☐   **17GSAP** General Services Administration Precursor Testing
            (GSAP test methods, FIPS 201)

☐   **17SCAP** Security Content Automation Protocol Testing
    (SCAP, CVE, CCE, CPE, CVSS, XCCDF and OVAL)

Figure A.2 provides a graphical representation of the list presented above. Also indicated are the dependencies and the compounding rules for the available test methods. For example, if the Cryptographic Hardware Modules – Hardware 2 (17CMH2) test is elected, the Cryptographic Hardware Modules – Hardware 1 testing (17CMH1), Cryptographic Algorithm Validation testing (17CAV) and Cryptographic and Security testing (17BCS) become mandatory prerequisites.

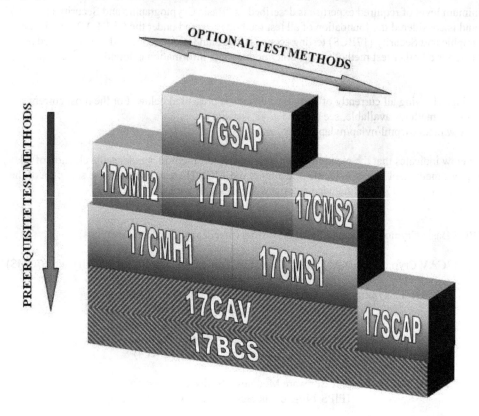

Legend:

17BCS   = Basic Cryptographic and Security Testing
17CAV   = Cryptographic Algorithm Validation Testing
17CMH1   = Cryptographic Modules – Hardware 1 Testing (Security Levels 1 to 3)
17CMH2   = Cryptographic Modules – Hardware 2 Testing (Security Levels 4 and above)
17CMS1   = Cryptographic Modules – Software 1 Testing (Security Levels 1 to 3)
17CMS2   = Cryptographic Modules – Software 2 Testing (Security Levels 4 and above)
17PIV   = Personal Identity Verification Testing
17GSAP   = GSA-Precursor Testing
17SCAP   = Security Content Automation Protocol Testing

Figure A.2. CST test methods.

Annex B

(normative)

Cryptographic Algorithms and Cryptographic Modules Testing

B.1   Additional general information

The CAVP and the CMVP are separate, collaborative programs based on a partnership between NIST's Computer Security Division and the Communication Security Establishment Canada (CSEC). The programs provide federal agencies—in the United States and Canada—confidence that a validated cryptographic algorithm has been implemented correctly and that a validated cryptographic module meets a claimed level of security assurance. The CAVP and the CMVP validate algorithms and modules used in a wide variety of products, including secure Internet browsers, secure radios, smart cards, space-based communications, munitions, security tokens, storage devices, and products supporting Public Key Infrastructure and electronic commerce. A module may be a stand-alone product such as a VPN, smartcard or toolkit or one module may be used in several products, so a small number of modules may be incorporated within hundreds of products. Likewise, the CAVP validates cryptographic algorithms that may be integrated in one or more cryptographic modules.

The two validation programs provide documented methodologies for conformance testing through defined sets of security requirements. For the CAVP, these are found in the individual validation system documents containing the validation test suites required to assure the algorithm has been implemented correctly The validation system documents are designed for each FIPS-Approved and NIST-Recommended cryptographic algorithm. For the CMVP, these security requirements are found in FIPS PUB 140-2, Security Requirements for Cryptographic Modules and the associated test metrics and methods in Derived Test Requirements for FIPS PUB 140-2, Security Requirements for Cryptographic Modules. The FIPS PUB 140-2 Annexes reference the underlying cryptographic algorithm standards or methods. Federal agencies are required to use modules that were validated as conforming to the provisions of FIPS PUB 140-2. The CMVP developed FIPS PUB 140-2 and the associated Derived Test Requirements to define the security requirements and test metrics and methods to ensure repeatability of tests and equivalency in results across the testing laboratories.

B.2   Scope of accreditation, test methods, additional references, terms and definitions

B.2.1   Scope of accreditation

NVLAP offers all interested laboratories a flexible, dynamic system of selecting a compound scope of accreditation under the CST LAP that best fits the laboratory's level of expertise and equipment.

The minimum level of required expertise is described as "Basic Cryptographic and Security (17BCS)" testing and is considered the foundation of all test methods covered under the CST LAP. The Basic Cryptographic and Security (17BCS) testing scope is not a stand-alone scope and it is mandated as a prerequisite for all other test methods.

The prerequisite required expertise for Cryptographic Module Hardware (17CMH) and Cryptographic Module Software (17CMS) test methods is Cryptographic Algorithm Validation Testing (17CAV). The 17CAV is not a stand-alone test method and is mandatory for 17CMH and/or 17CMS testing. 17CMS can be selected independently of 17CMH testing. If only 17CMS methods are selected above 17CAV, only the testing of software modules can be performed (i.e. no firmware, hardware, hybrid modules or if FIPS 140-2 Section 4.5 is selected as spplicable). Testing of firmware or hybrid modules requires selection of both 17CMH and 17CMS test methods.

NOTE   Firmware and hybrid modules are defined in FIPS 140-1 and supporting documents or their successors.

B.2.2   Test methods

B.2.2.1   General

For each testing program, the test methods are listed below. When a hierarchically higher test method is elected, all test methods associated with the prerequisite scopes also become mandatory.

B.2.2.2   Cryptographic Algorithm Validation Testing (17CAV)

The minimum level of required expertise for the 17CMS and 17CMH test methods is described as Cryptographic Algorithm Validation Testing (17CAV). This is considered the foundation of 17CMS and 17CMH testing. The 17CAV test is not a stand-alone test method and is mandatory for 17CMS and 17CMH testing.

17CAV/01   NIST - Cryptographic Algorithm Validation Testing (CAV) for all FIPS-approved and/or NIST-recommended security functions as required in FIPS 140-2 Annexes (and all superseded versions) – see http://csrc nist.gov/groups/STM/cavp/index html.

B.2.2.3   Cryptographic Software Modules – Software 1 Testing (17CMS1)

17CMS1/01   All test methods in accordance with FIPS 140-1 and its successors for Security Levels 1 to 3, except those listed in 17CMS2/01.

NOTE   The 17CMS1/01 test methods for FIPS 140-1 are not available for new modules but only for modules that have been already validated and must be retested for reasons outside the scope of this document.

B.2.2.4   Cryptographic Software Modules – Software 2 Testing (17CMS2)

17CMS2/01   Test methods for Software Security Level 4, in accordance with FIPS 140-1 and its successors.

NOTE   The 17CMS2/01 test methods for FIPS 140-1 are not available for new modules but only for modules that have been already validated and must be retested for reasons outside the scope of this document.

B.2.2.5   Cryptographic Hardware Modules – Hardware 1 Testing (17CMH1)

17CMH1/01   All test methods in accordance with FIPS 140-1 and its successors for Security Levels 1 to 3, except those listed in 17CMH2/01.

NOTE   The 17CMH1/01 test methods for FIPS 140-1 are not available for new modules but only for modules that have been already validated and must be retested for reasons outside the scope of this document.

B.2.2.6   Cryptographic Hardware Modules – Hardware 2 Testing (17CMH2)

17CMH2/01   Test methods for Physical Security Level 4, in accordance with FIPS 140-1 and its successors.

NOTE   The 17CMH2/01 test methods for FIPS 140-1 are not available for new modules but only for modules that have been already validated and must be retested for reasons outside the scope of this document.

B.2.3   Additional references for Cryptographic Algorithms and Cryptographic Modules Testing

— Federal Information Processing Standards Publication FIPS PUB 140-1, *Security Requirements for Cryptographic Modules* (see http://csrc nist.gov/publications/fips/fips140-1/fips1401.pdf)

— Federal Information Processing Standards Publication FIPS 140-2, *Security Requirements for Cryptographic Modules*, and successors
(see http://csrc nist.gov/publications/fips/fips140-2/fips1402.pdf)

— A Comparison of the Security Requirements for Cryptographic Modules in FIPS 140-1 and FIPS 140-2 (see http://csrc nist.gov/publications/nistpubs/800-29/sp800-29.pdf)

— Derived Test Requirements for FIPS 140-1
(see http://csrc nist.gov/groups/STM/cmvp/documents/fips140-1/1401test.pdf)

— Derived Test Requirements (DTR) for FIPS 140-1 APPENDIX A, *A Cryptographic Module Security Policy* (see http://csrc nist.gov/groups/STM/cmvp/documents/fips140-1/1401testA.pdf)

— Implementation Guidance for FIPS 140-1 and the Cryptographic Module Validation Program (see http://csrc nist.gov/groups/STM/cmvp/documents/fips140-1/FIPS1401IG.pdf)

— Annex A: Approved Security Functions for FIPS 140-2, *Security Requirements for Cryptographic Modules* (see http://csrc.nist.gov/publications/fips/fips140-2/fips1402annexa.pdf)

— Annex B: Approved Protection Profiles for FIPS 140-2, *Security Requirements for Cryptographic Modules* (see http://csrc.nist.gov/publications/fips/fips140-2/fips1402annexb.pdf)

— Annex C: Approved Random Number Generators for FIPS 140-2, *Security Requirements for Cryptographic Modules* (see http://csrc nist.gov/publications/fips/fips140-2/fips1402annexc.pdf)

— Annex D: Approved Key Establishment Techniques for FIPS 140-2, *Security Requirements for Cryptographic Modules* (see http://csrc nist.gov/publications/fips/fips140-2/fips1402annexd.pdf)

— *Derived Test Requirements [DTR] for FIPS PUB 140-2 Security Requirements for Cryptographic Modules* (see http://csrc.nist.gov/groups/STM/cmvp/documents/fips140-2/FIPS1402DTR.pdf)

— Implementation Guidance for FIPS 140-2 and the Cryptographic Module Validation Program. (see http://csrc nist.gov/groups/STM/cmvp/documents/fips140-2/FIPS1402IG.pdf)

— Cryptographic Algorithm Validation Program Management Manual
(see http://csrc nist.gov/groups/STM/cavp/documents/CAVPMM.pdf)

— Frequently Asked Questions for the Cryptographic Algorithm Validation Program Concerning the Validation of Cryptographic Algorithm Implementations (see http://csrc.nist.gov/groups/STM/cavp/documents/CAVPFAQ.pdf)

— Frequently Asked Questions for the Cryptographic Module Validation Program (see http://csrc.nist.gov/groups/STM/cmvp/documents/CMVPFAQ.pdf)

— Cryptographic Module Validation Program Management Manual (see http://csrc.nist.gov/groups/STM/cmvp/documents/CMVPMM.pdf)

B.2.4   Additional terms and definitions

B.2.4.1
CAVS
Cryptographic Algorithm Validation System Test Documentation Tool.

B.2.4.2
CRYPTIK
Cryptographic Module Validation Requirements Test Documentation Tool.

B.2.4.3
METRIX
CMVP and CAVP Programmatic Metrics Collection Program.

B.3   Additional accreditation process requirements

B.3.1   Additional accreditation requirements

B.3.1.1   Additional Accreditation Requirements for the 17CAV Testing

United States federal laboratories are prohibited from applying for accreditation to 17CAV and those related test methods based on 17CAV to avoid conflict of interest with the validation authority.

In order for an applicant laboratory to qualify for any of the Cryptographic Algorithm testing, the laboratory shall achieve accreditation by NVLAP in the Basic Cryptographic and Security Testing (17BCS).

B.3.1.2   Additional Accreditation Requirements for the 17CMH1 and 17CMS1 Testing

In order for an applicant laboratory to qualify for any of the Cryptographic Modules – Hardware and/or Software testing, (17CMH1 and/or 17CMS1), the laboratory shall achieve accreditation by NVLAP in the Cryptographic Algorithm Validation Testing (17CAV) test method.

B.3.2   Additional activities prior to an on-site assessment

There are no requirements additional to those provided in clause 3.2 of this handbook.

B.3.3   Additional on-site assessment requirements

There are no requirements additional to those provided in clause 3.3 of this handbook.

B.3.4 Additional proficiency testing requirements

B.3.4.1 General

A proficiency testing artifact (Clause 3.1.2b) is the final step in the initial accreditation process for the 17CMH1, 17CMH2, 17CMS1 and 17CMS2 test methods. The artifact is a cryptographic module developed by the CMVP for laboratory testing for conformance to FIPS 140-1 and supporting documents, or successors. The artifact conformance testing will demonstrate the laboratories knowledge of the supporting standards as applied in an actual implementation, knowledge of the programmatically required test methods and metrics, and the laboratories testing skills and use of appropriate tools.

During the testing process, the proficiency artifact will also mimic the relationship a laboratory will have with a module vendor and the CMVP in following up with questions and guidance as the proficiency artifact design and documentation may be purposely incomplete or non-compliant. All these elements are brought together with the submission of the proficiency artifact test report to the CMVP using the CRYPTIK tool. The time frame for completion of the testing is determined by the laboratory. The laboratory test report submission shall demonstrate that the laboratory is familiar with the entire testing and reporting process.

The validation program may also use a proficiency artifact as part of the renewal process once accreditation is granted.

NVLAP, in collaboration with all CST validation programs, considers the validation reports submitted to the validation programs as ongoing proficiency tests. A large number of flaws in the reports submitted to any of the validation programs can trigger the laboratory's suspension or revocation of the accreditation. For more information see 3.10 of this handbook.

B.3.4.2 Additional proficiency testing requirements for the 17CAV testing

There are no requirements additional to those provided in clause 3.4 of this handbook.

B.3.4.3 Additional proficiency testing requirements for the 17CMH and17CMS testing

There are no requirements additional to those provided in clause 3.4 of this handbook.

B.4 Additional management requirements for accreditation

There are no requirements additional to those provided in clause 4 of this handbook.

B.5 Additional technical requirements for accreditation

B.5.1 General

There are no requirements additional to those provided in Section 5.1 of this handbook.

B.5.2   Additional personnel requirements

B.5.2.1   General

For a laboratory to qualify for accreditation under the CST LAP, the laboratory shall demonstrate, in addition to the technical expertise required by each test method as described below, that their personnel has basic knowledge of cryptographic and security practice for information systems and that the laboratory is aware of the governing standards and publications, especially the ones listed in this handbook.

B.5.2.2   Additional personnel requirements for the 17CAV, 17CMH and17CMS testing

The laboratory's personnel shall have experience or be trained prior to accreditation in the areas of:

a)   17CAV, 17CMH, and 17CMS:

    1)   knowledge of Validation Program's programmatic guidance and management documents;
    2)   familiarity with the cryptographic algorithms listed in FIPS 140-2 Annexes;
    3)   familiarity with random bit generators and entropy requirements;
    4)   familiarity with key establishment methods and concepts;
    5)   familiarity with Approved modes of operation;
    6)   specification of the module (e.g. hardware, software, hybrid and/or firmware);
    7)   familiarity with module ports and interfaces;
    8)   familiarity with trusted path and direct entry methods;
    9)   specification of roles and services;
    10)   familiarity with authentication methods (role and identity-based) and strengths;
    11)   familiarity with bypass mechanisms and concepts;
    12)   finite state machine model analysis;
    13)   familiarity with development of test jigs, software debuggers, binary editors, compilers, and software diagnostic tools;
    14)   software design specifications, including high-level languages;
    15)   familiarity with operating systems and concepts (e.g. Microsoft, UNIX, LINUX, ARM, Apple, etc.);
    16)   key management techniques and concepts;
    17)   zeroization methods;
    18)   key entry and output;
    19)   familiarity with the cryptographic protocols including, but not limited to, SSL, TLS, IKE, SSH, OTAR, etc.;
    20)   familiarity with FCC EMI/EMC Class A and Class B requirements and intentional emitters such as radio devices;
    21)   familiarity with cryptographic self-test techniques, including but not limited to, power-up, conditional tests, known answer tests, integrity tests, load and bypass tests, etc.;
    22)   familiarity with Design Assurance such as configuration management, delivery, operation, and development;
    23)   familiarity with mitigation of other attack mechanisms; and
    24)   familiarity with Security Policy requirements (e.g. FIPS 140-2 Appendix C).

b)   17 CMH1 Security Levels 1 to 3:

    1)   production grade, tamper evident, and tamper detection techniques;

2) familiarity with hardware implementations and technologies associated with single-chip and multi-chip embodiments;

3) familiarity with epoxies, potting materials, adhesives (e.g. tamper evident labels) and their chemical properties;

4) familiarity with electrical design, schematics and concepts including logic design and HDL representations; and

5) familiarity with skills associated with tamper mitigation methods and performing test methods of compromising tamper protection mechanisms.

c) 17CMH2 Security Level 4:

1) familiarity with voltage and temperature measurement (Environmental Failure Protection/Environmental Failure Testing (EFP/EFT);

2) familiarity with tamper detection/response envelopes; and

3) familiarity with formal modeling methods.

d) 17 CMS1 Security Levels 1 to 3:

1) familiarity with evaluated operating systems under the Common Criteria EAL2 through EAL3 or equivalents.

e) 17CMS2 Security Level 4:

1) familiarity with formal modeling methods; and

2) familiarity with evaluated operating systems under the Common Criteria EAL4 or equivalent.

B.5.3   Additional accommodation and environmental conditions

B.5.3.1   General

The laboratory should have appropriate areas, including ventilation and safety, for the use of test methods using chemical solvents and heating/cooling apparatus.

B.5.3.2   Additional accommodation and environmental requirements for the 17CAV, 17CMH and 17CMS testing

Implementations-under-test, IUT specific documentation, IUT specific test jigs, harnesses, supporting test apparatus or test results, shall be protected from persons outside the laboratory, from visitors to the laboratory, from laboratory personnel without a need to know, and from other unauthorized persons.

B.5.4   Additional test and calibration methods and method validation

There are no requirements additional to those provided in 5.4.

B.5.5   Additional equipment requirements for the 17CAV, 17CMH and17CMS testing

B.5.5.1   General

The laboratory applying for accreditation for the 17CAV, 17CMH or 17CMS testing shall own at least one designated workstation and compatible operating system that will run the CAVS, *CRYPTIK,*and *METRIX* tools. The workstation or other designated workstation shall have internet access and e-mail capability (for report submission). Workstations shall have Interfaces for loading images from a digital camera and acquiring scanned document images and/or hard copy printouts. Workstations must have sufficient storage capability, performance and features as specified by the tool provider.

B.5.5.2   The laboratory shall also meet the following minimum hardware and software requirements:

a) Hardware: Security Levels 1 to 3:

   1)   at least 40 GB of available space on the hard drive;
   2)   X-Acto "Type" knives (including various blades);
   3)   strong artificial light source (Wavelength range of 400 nm to 750 nm);
   4)   magnifying glass;
   5)   Dremmel[1] "Type" rotary tool (including accessory bits: cutting, grinding, drilling, carving, etc.);
   6)   jeweler's screwdrivers (e.g., flat, Phillips, Robertson, torx, hex key);
   7)   dentist picks and mirrors;
   8)   hobbyist saw;
   9)   small pliers (e.g., needle nose, standard nose, long nose, curved nose, side cutters);
   10) hammer;
   11) chisels;
   12) fine (small) files or rasps;
   13) hair dryer/ heat source;
   14) Volt-Ohm-Meter (VOM) or Digital Multi-Meter (DMM) (basic functions to include an ammeter, voltmeter and ohmmeter): calibration only required as needed on the test method employed;
   15) digital camera with flash and MACRO (near focus) features;
   16) digital scanner;
   17) printer; and
   18) miscellaneous protection equipment for chemical testing (e.g., goggles, gloves) – optional.

b) Hardware: Security Level 4:

   1)   variable power supply;
   2)   temperature chamber (procured, rented, or leased, as needed);
   3)   digital storage oscilloscope or logic analyzer (procured, rented, or leased, as needed); and
   4)   Reference Text: Formal Model text (Z).

c) Software: Security Levels 1 to 3:

   1)   appropriate compilers, debuggers, and binary editors;
   2)   a Validation Program-originated copy of *CRYPTIK* (latest version);
   3)   a Validation Program-originated copy of *CAVS* (latest version);
   4)   a Validation Program-originated copy of *METRIX* (latest version);
   5)   Microsoft Office Professional (Microsoft Word and Access);
   6)   Adobe Acrobat Standard (pdf generation tool); and
   7)   a Validation program supplied or designated file or e-mail encryption application.

---

[1] Certain commercial entities, equipment, or materials may be identified in this document in order to describe a requirement adequately. Such identification is not intended to imply recommendation or endorsement by NIST.

d) Software: Security Level 4:

    1)   Reference Text: Formal Model text (Z)

B.5.6   Additional measurement traceability

B.5.6.1   Additional general requirements

There are no requirements additional to those provided in 5.6.1 of this handbook.

B.5.6.2   Additional calibration requirements

There are no requirements additional to those provided in 5.6.2. of this handbook.

B.5.6.3   Additional testing requirements for the 17CAV, 17CMH and 17CMS testing

Traceability to the requirements in the FIPS 140-1 (or successors) is achieved via the assertions, the associated DTRs documents and the CAVS and *CRYPTIK* test reporting tool. The DTRs are divided into two sets of requirements: one levied on the vendor and one levied on the tester of the cryptographic module.

Test vectors and results for cryptographic algorithm testing shall be generated and checked using the provided CAVS tool.

Laboratories shall use the test methods described in the document *Derived Test Requirements for FIPS PUB 140-1, Security Requirements for Cryptographic Modules* (or successor), with clarifications provided in the document *Implementation Guidance for FIPS PUB 140-1 and the Cryptographic Module Validation Program* (or successor).

When exceptions are deemed necessary for technical reasons, the validation authority (CAVP and/or CMVP) shall be informed and details shall be described in the test report. The laboratory should submit a Request for Guidance (RFG) to document and received official guidance from the validation programs. When the *CRYPTIK* tool cannot support submission of the test result information, the laboratory shall provide documentation to ensure that the correct interpretation of the test assertions is maintained. When necessary, laboratory's reports may be used to update *CRYPTIK* and the accompanying documentation. The *CRYPTIK* tool shall not be distributed, provided, or used by anyone other than laboratory personnel.

Laboratories shall use the test methods and tests for the security functions listed at the websites: http://csrc nist.gov/groups/STM/cavp/index html, and http://csrc nist.gov/groups/STM/cmvp/index.html.

When testing is performed at the vendor site or other mutually agreed upon site, only the laboratory personnel shall use or have access to the CAVS, *CRYPTIK*, or *METRIX* tools supplied by the validation program.

B.5.7   Additional sampling requirements

There are no requirements additional to those provided in 5.7 of this handbook.

B.5.8   Additional handling of test and calibration items requirements

There are no requirements additional to those provided in 5.8 of this handbook.

B.5.9   Additional assuring the quality of test and calibration results requirements

There are no requirements additional to those provided in 5.9 of this handbook.

B.5.10   Additional reporting the results requirements

The CAVS tool shall be used for 17CAV test report submission.   The *CRYPTIK* tool shall be used for the 17 CMH and 17CMS test report submission.   The *METRIX* tool shall be used to submit quarterly, or as specified by the validation program, results of test statistics.

Annex C

(normative)

Personal Identity Verification (PIV) Testing

C.1   Additional general information

NIST established the NIST Personal Identity Verification Program (NPIVP) to validate Personal Identity Verification (PIV) components required by FIPS 201 within ITL. NVLAP accredits NPIVP laboratories for testing of PIV Card Application and PIV Middleware implementations for conformance to the NIST SP 800-73, Interfaces for Personal Identity Verification, which is normatively referenced from FIPS 201. The Personal Identity Verification (PIV) objectives to validating PIV components by NPIVP are:

- to validate the conformance of two PIV components: PIV Middleware and PIV Card Application with the specifications in NIST SP 800-73-1 or successors; and

- to provide assurance that the set of PIV Middleware and PIV Card Applications that have been validated by NPIVP are interoperable.

C.2   Scope of accreditation, test methods, additional references, terms and definitions

C.2.1   Scope of accreditation

NVLAP offers all interested laboratories a flexible, dynamic system of selecting a compound scope of accreditation under the CST LAP that best fits the laboratory's level of expertise and equipment.

The minimum level of required expertise is described as "Basic Cryptographic and Security (17BCS)" testing and is considered the foundation of all test methods covered under the CST LAP. The Basic Cryptographic and Security (17BCS) testing scope is not a stand-alone scope and it is mandated as a prerequisite for all other test methods.

The prerequisite required expertise for Personal Identity Verification Testing (17PIV) test methods also requires selection of 17CAV, 17CMH1 and 17CMS1 test methods.

C.2.2   Test methods

C.2.2.1   General

For each testing program, the test methods are listed below. When a hierarchically higher test method is elected, all test methods associated with the prerequisite scopes also become mandatory.

C.2.2.2   Personal Identity Verification Testing (17PIV)

The 17PIV testing is not a stand-alone test method. It requires, the Cryptographic Software module - Software 1 (17CMS1) test as well as Cryptographic Hardware Module - Hardware 1 (17CMH1) test, Cryptographic Algorithm Validation test (17CAV), and Basic Cryptographic and Security Testing (17BCS) as prerequisites.

Further, both test methods (17PIV/01 and 17PIV/02) are required for accreditation in the PIV Testing Program.

17PIV/01 PIV Card Applications Conformance Test Suite for products meeting specifications in the FIPS 201 and NIST Special Publication 800-73 or successors.

17PIV/02 PIV Middleware Conformance Test Suite for products meeting specifications in the FIPS 201 and NIST Special Publication 800-73 or successors.

C.2.3 Additional references for the Personal Identity Verification Testing (17PIV)

C.2.3.1 Federal Information Processing Standards

— FIPS 201 or successors, *Personal Identity Verification of Governmental Employees and Contractors*, 2005 or successor, http://csrc nist.gov/publications/fips/fips201-1/FIPS-201-1-chng1.pdf.

C.2.3.2 NIST Special Publications (SP) and tools for PIV

NOTE All NIST Special Publications (SP) listed below are available for download at the following site: http://csrc nist.gov/publications/PubsSPs html.

— NIST SP 800-21-1, *Guideline for Implementing Cryptography in the Federal Government*, second edition, NIST, December 2005 or latest (http://csrc nist.gov/publications/nistpubs/800-21-1/sp800-21-1 Dec2005.pdf)

— NIST SP 800-56A, *Recommendation for Pair-Wise Key Establishment Schemes using Discrete Logarithm Cryptography, General*, NIST, March 2007 (http://csrc.nist.gov/publications/nistpubs/800-56A/SP800-56A Revision1 Mar08-2007.pdf)

— NIST SP 800-57, *Recommendation for Key Management - Part 1, General*, NIST, March 2007 (http://csrc nist.gov/publications/nistpubs/800-57/sp800-57-Part1-revised2 Mar08-2007.pdf)

— NIST SP 800-57, *Recommendation for Key Management - Part 2, Best Practices for Key Management Organization*, NIST, August 2005 or latest (http://csrc nist.gov/publications/nistpubs/800-57/SP800-57-Part2.pdf)

— NIST SP 800-73 (Revision 3: 800-73-3), *Interfaces for Personal Identity Verification*, NIST, February 2010 or latest

— NIST SP 800-76, *Biometric Data Specification for Personal Identity Verification*, NIST, January 2007 or latest (http://csrc nist.gov/publications/nistpubs/800-76-1/SP800-76-1 012407.pdf)

— NIST SP 800-78 or successors, *Cryptographic Standards and Key Sizes for Personal Identity Verification*, NIST, April 2005 or latest (http://csrc.nist.gov/publications/nistpubs)

— NIST SP 800-79, *Guidelines for the Certification and Accreditation of PIV Card Issuing Organizations*, NIST, June 2008 or latest (http://csrc.nist.gov/publications/nistpubs/800-79-1/SP800-79-1.pdf)

— NIST SP 800-85A-2, *PIV Card Application and Middleware Interface Test Guidelines*, NIST, July 2010 or later (http://csrc nist.gov/publications/nistpubs/800-85A-2/sp800-85A-2-final.pdf)

— NIST SP 800-96, or successor, *PIV Card / Reader Interoperability Guidelines*, NIST, September 2006 or later (http://csrc nist.gov/publications/nistpubs/800-96/SP800-96-091106.pdf)

— PIV Card Application and Middleware Test Runner for NPIVP

C.2.3.3 ISO/IEC standards for PIV

— ISO/IEC 7810

— ISO/IEC 7816

— ISO/IEC 14443

C.2.4 Additional terms and definitions

There are no additional terms and definitions to those provided in Section 1.5 of this handbook.

C.3 Additional accreditation process requirements

C.3.1 Additional accreditation requirements for the 17PIV Testing

All laboratories applying for the test methods associated with 17PIV testing shall be based in North America. The cryptographic modules in the PIV systems (both on-card and issuer software) are required to be validated to FIPS 140-2 or successors with an overall Security Level 2 (or higher) while the cryptographic module on the PIV card is required to provide physical Security Level 3 to protect the PIV private keys in storage.

As such, in order for an applicant laboratory to qualify for any of the Personal Identification Verification testing, the laboratory shall achieve accreditation by NVLAP in the Cryptographic and Security testing (17BCS), Cryptographic Algorithm Validation Testing (17CAV), Cryptographic Hardware Module Testing (17CMH1) and Cryptographic Software Module Testing (17CMS1).

Further, the applicant laboratory cannot choose only one (17PIV/01 or 17PIV/02) test method. Both test methods must be elected in order to qualify for 17 PIV testing.

C.3.2 Additional activities prior to an on-site assessment

There are no requirements additional to those provided in clause 3.2 of this handbook.

C.3.3 Additional on-site assessment requirements

There are no requirements additional to those provided in clause 3.3 of this handbook.

C.3.4 Additional proficiency testing requirements

C.3.4.1 General

NVLAP, in collaboration with all CST validation programs, considers the validation reports submitted to the validation programs as ongoing proficiency tests. A large number of flaws in the reports submitted to any of the validation programs can trigger the laboratory's suspension or revocation of the accreditation. For more information see 3.10 of this handbook.

C.3.4.2 Additional proficiency testing requirements for the 17PIV testing

Proficiency testing for the 17PIV tests will require proof of the laboratory's ability to handle the *PIV Card Application* and *PIV Middleware* (NIST SP 800-85A) test tools, provided by NIST/ITL or NVLAP. The laboratory shall demonstrate that all appropriate personnel are familiar with the tools, are capable of configuring the tools, running the conformance tests, verifying the results and generating the report.

C.4 Additional management requirements for accreditation

There are no requirements additional to those provided in clause 4 of this handbook.

C.5 Additional technical requirements for accreditation

C.5.1 General

There are no requirements additional to those provided in Section 5.1 of this handbook.

C.5.2 Additional personnel requirements

C.5.2.1 General

For a laboratory to qualify for accreditation under the CST LAP, the laboratory shall demonstrate, in addition to the technical expertise required by each test method as described below, that their personnel has basic knowledge of cryptographic and security practice for information systems and that the laboratory is aware of the governing standards and publications, especially the ones listed in this handbook.

C.5.2.2 Additional personnel requirements for the for the 17PIV testing

The laboratory's personnel shall have experience or be trained prior to accreditation in the areas of:

a) cryptography - symmetric versus asymmetric algorithms and uses;

b) cryptography - encryption protocols and implementations;

c) key management techniques and concepts;

d) cryptographic self-test techniques;

e) familiarity with the families of cryptographic algorithms;

f) FIPS-approved and NIST-recommended security functions (FIPS 140-2 or successors);

g)   cryptography - Public Key Infrastructure (PKI);

h)   access control security models;

i)   smart cards;

j)   smart card readers (contact and contactless);

k)   Application Protocol Data Unit (APDU);

l)   Basic Encoding Rules (BER);

m)   biometric authentication techniques;

n)   concepts of the operational PIV systems; and

o)   contact and contactless interface standards.

C.5.3   Additional accommodation and environmental conditions

There are no requirements additional to those provided in 5.3.

C.5.4   Additional test and calibration methods and method validation

There are no requirements additional to those provided in 5.4.

C.5.5   Additional equipment requirements for the 17PIV testing

C.5.5.1   The laboratory applying for accreditation for the 17PIV testing shall own at least one designated IBM compatible PC[1] equipped with, at minimum, a compact disk rewritable (CD-RW) drive or other secure digital storage media and running Microsoft Windows XP[1] (or later) or compatible.

C.5.5.2   The laboratory shall also meet the following minimum hardware, software, and operating system requirements for the platform on which the *PIV Card Application* and *PIV Middleware* tools (also known as *PIV Test Runner*) will run:

a)   Hardware:

1)   a test computer running Windows XP[1] and with at least 4 MB of available space on the hard disk;
2)   contact and contactless smart card reader or a dual interface reader;
3)   a dual interface FIPS 201 conformant PIV card loaded with SP 800-73 conformant PIV card application; and
4)   a printer for reporting and documenting the test results.

b)   Software:

1)   SUN[1] Microsystems Java Runtime Environment (JRE) version 1.5 or later;
2)   *Java Cryptography Extension* (JCE) Unlimited Strength Jurisdiction Policy Files 5.0; and
3)   *PIV Card Application* and *PIV Middleware* test toolkit application software provided by NIST/ITL or NVLAP (version 2.9.8 or later).

---

[1] Certain commercial entities, equipment, or materials may be identified in this document in order to describe a requirement adequately. Such identification is not intended to imply recommendation or endorsement by NIST.

C.5.6   Additional measurement traceability

C.5.6.1   Additional general requirements

There are no requirements additional to those provided in 5.6.1 of this handbook.

C.5.6.2   Additional calibration requirements

There are no requirements additional to those provided in 5.6.2 of this handbook.

C.5.6.3   Additional testing requirements for the 17PIV testing

Laboratories shall use the test methods and tests listed in the NIST SP 800-85A: *PIV Card Application and Middleware Interface Test Guidelines* (or successors) for conformance testing of the PIV card application and PIV middleware. For additional clarifications, check the documentation listed on the NPIVP website < http://csrc.nist.gov/groups/SNS/piv/index.html>.

FIPS 201 Appendix B.3 specifies that a PIV system/component is "FIPS 201-compliant" after each of IUT's constituent parts have met individual validation requirements. For a PIV card, the constituent parts requiring validation include:

- PIV card application validation for conformance to NIST SP 800-73 through NPIVP; and
- cryptographic module validation for FIPS 140-2 Security Requirements for Cryptographic Modules (or successors) conformance of the cryptographic module that hosts the PIV card application.

Annex D
(normative)

General Services Administration Precursor (GSAP) Testing

D.1   Additional general information

The FIPS 201 Evaluation Program (EP) is a U.S. Government entity administered by the Office of Government-wide Policy (OGP), within the General Services Administration (GSA) agency. The goal of the FIPS 201 Evaluation Program (EP) is to evaluate products and services against the requirements outlined in FIPS 201 and its supporting documents. In addition to derived test requirements developed to test conformance to the National Institute of Standards and Technology (NIST) Standard, GSA has also established interoperability and performance metrics to further determine product suitability. In order to facilitate testing these requirements, the EP has developed a set of approval and test procedures for 33 Product Categories, which outline the evaluation criteria, approval mechanisms and test process employed by the laboratory during its evaluation of a supplier's product or service against the requirements for that category. The EP Laboratories (EPLs) utilize these approval procedures and test procedures to test Products for FIPS 201 conformance.

D.2   Scope of accreditation, test methods, additional references, terms and definitions

D.2.1   Scope of accreditation

NVLAP offers all interested laboratories a flexible, dynamic system of selecting a compound scope of accreditation under the CST LAP that best fits the laboratory's level of expertise and equipment.

The minimum level of required expertise is described as "Basic Cryptographic and Security (17BCS)" testing and is considered the foundation of all test methods covered under the CST LAP. The Basic Cryptographic and Security (17BCS) testing scope is not a stand-alone scope and it is mandated as a prerequisite for all other test methods

The prerequisite required expertise for General Services Administration Precursor (17GSAP) test methods also requires selection of the 17PIV test methods.

D.2.2   Test methods

D.2.2.1   General

For each testing program, the test methods are listed below. When a hierarchically higher test method is elected, all test methods associated with the prerequisite scopes also become mandatory.

D.2.2.2   General Services Administration Precursor Testing (17GSAP)

17GSAP/01   FIPS 201 Evaluation Program – Electromagnetically Opaque Sleeve

17GSAP/02   FIPS 201 Evaluation Program – Electronic Personalization

17GSAP/03   FIPS 201 Evaluation Program – PIV Card

17GSAP/04   FIPS 201 Evaluation Program – PIV Card Reader - Authentication Key

17GSAP/05   FIPS 201 Evaluation Program – PIV Card Reader - Biometric

17GSAP/06   FIPS 201 Evaluation Program – PIV Card Reader - CHUID (Contact)

17GSAP/07   FIPS 201 Evaluation Program – PIV Card Reader - CHUID (Contactless)

17GSAP/08   FIPS 201 Evaluation Program – PIV Card Reader - Transparent

17GSAP/09   FIPS 201 Evaluation Program – Template Generator

17GSAP/10   FIPS 201 Evaluation Program – Card Printer Station

17GSAP/11   FIPS 201 Evaluation Program – PIV Card Reader - CHUID Authentication (Contact)

17GSAP/12   FIPS 201 Evaluation Program – PIV Card Reader - CHUID Authentication (Contactless)

17GSAP/13   FIPS 201 Evaluation Program – Graphical Personalization

17GSAP/14   FIPS 201 Evaluation Program – Facial Image Capturing Camera

17GSAP/15   FIPS 201 Evaluation Program – Biometric Authentication System

17GSAP/16   FIPS 201 Evaluation Program – CAK Authentication System

17GSAP/17   FIPS 201 Evaluation Program – Certificate Validator

17GSAP/18   FIPS 201 Evaluation Program – Certificate Validator (without authentication)

17GSAP/19   FIPS 201 Evaluation Program – Card Reader – Biometric Authentication

17GSAP/20   FIPS 201 Evaluation Program – CHUID Authentication System

17GSAP/21   FIPS 201 Evaluation Program – Facial Image Capturing (Middleware)

17GSAP/22   FIPS 201 Evaluation Program – PIV Authentication System

17GSAP/23   FIPS 201 Evaluation Program – SCVP Client

17GSAP/24   FIPS 201 Evaluation Program – SCVP Client (without authentication)

D.2.3   Additional references for General Services Administration Precursor Testing (17GSAP)

— HSPD 12, *Policy for a Common Identification Standard for Federal Employees and Contractors*, August 27, 2004, http://www.dhs.gov/xabout/laws/gc_1217616624097.shtm

— NIST SP 800-85B, *PIV Data Model Conformance Test Guidelines*, NIST, September 2009, http://csrc.nist.gov/publications/drafts/800-85B-1/draft-sp800-85B-1.pdf

— FIPS 201 Evaluation Program – Authentication Key Reader Test Procedure, v 4.0.0.0 or later

— FIPS 201 Evaluation Program – Biometric Reader Test Procedure, v 4.0.0 or later

— FIPS 201 Evaluation Program – CHUID Reader (Contact) Test Procedure, v 4.0.0 or later

— FIPS 201 Evaluation Program – CHUID Reader (Contactless) Test Procedure, v 4.0.0 or later

— FIPS 201 Evaluation Program – CHUID Authentication Reader (Contact) Test Procedure, v 2.0.0 or later

— FIPS 201 Evaluation Program – CHUID Authentication Reader (Contactless) Test Procedure, v 2.0.0 or later

— FIPS 201 Evaluation Program – Electromagnetically Opaque Sleeve Test Procedure, v 3.0.0 or later

— FIPS 201 Evaluation Program – Electronic Personalization Test Procedure, v 5.0.0 or later

— FIPS 201 Evaluation Program – PIV Card Test Procedure, v 3.0.0 or later

— FIPS 201 Evaluation Program – Template Generator Test Procedure, v 2.0.0 or later

— FIPS 201 Evaluation Program – Transparent Card Reader Test Procedure, v 5.0.0 or later

— FIPS 201 Evaluation Program – Graphical Personalization Test Procedure, v 1.0.0 or later

— FIPS 201 Evaluation Program – Facial Image Capturing Camera Test Procedure, v 1.0.0 or later

— FIPS 201 Evaluation Program – Card Printer Station Test Procedure, v 2.0.0 or later

— FIPS 201 Evaluation Program – Biometric Authentication System Test Procedure, v 1.0.0 or later

— FIPS 201 Evaluation Program – CAK Authentication System Test Procedure, v 1.0.0 or later

— FIPS 201 Evaluation Program – Certificate Validator Test Procedure, v 3.0.0 or later

— FIPS 201 Evaluation Program – Certificate Validator (without authentication) Test Procedure, v 2.0.0 or later

— FIPS 201 Evaluation Program – Biometric Authentication Card Reader Test Procedure, v 1.0.0 or later

— FIPS 201 Evaluation Program – CHUID Authentication System Test Procedure, v 1.0.0 or later

— FIPS 201 Evaluation Program – Facial Image Capturing Middleware Test Procedure, v 1.0.0 or later

— FIPS 201 Evaluation Program – PIV Authentication System Test Procedure, v 1.0.0 or later

— FIPS 201 Evaluation Program – SCVP Client Test Procedure, v 2.0.0 or later

— FIPS 201 Evaluation Program – SCVP Client (without authentication) Test Procedure, v 1.0.0 or later

NOTE   The most current version of the documents listed above can be downloaded from the GSA's website: http://fips201ep.cio.gov/ (click on the "Test Procedures" link).

D.2.4   Additional terms and definitions

D.2.4.1
GSA FIPS 201 EP
U.S. Government entity responsible for ensuring that products are validated against FIPS 201 and it's supporting requirements. The EP is administered by the Office of Government-wide Policy (OGP), within the General Services Administration (GSA) agency.

D.2.4.2
EP Laboratories (EPLs)
Accredited laboratories that are authorized to perform FIPS 201 conformance testing on products submitted by vendors. The EPLs perform testing in accordance with GSA FIPS 201 EP approval procedures and test procedures.

D.2.4.3
Approved FIPS 201 Products and Services List (APL)
A list of qualified products that have been validated for FIPS-201 conformance.

D.2.4.4
Removed Products List (RPL)
A list of products that are not longer conformant with requirements specified in the FIPS 201-1 and its supporting documents. When APL products become non-conformant, they are placed on the RPL.

D.2.4.5
Central Certificate Validator (CCV)
A free service hosted by GSA that can be used to determine if a presented identity credential (PKI certificate) is valid, i.e., was legitimately issued and has not expired or been terminated. The CCV uses the processes of path discovery and path validation to verify the binding between the subject identifier and the subject public key in the certificate.

D.3   Additional accreditation process requirements

D.3.1   Additional accreditation requirements for the 17GSAP Testing

In order for an applicant laboratory to qualify as a General Services Administration (GSA) FIPS 201 Evaluation Laboratory, the laboratory shall achieve accreditation by NVLAP in the GSA FIPS 201 test methods (17GSAP), including all 17GSAP/xx test methods listed herein, or the updated list from the CST LAP website. Before the laboratory qualifies to apply to GSA as a GSA FIPS 201 Evaluation Program laboratory (GSA EP), the laboratory shall prove to GSA that the laboratory can perform all evaluations for all FIPS 201 categories of products and services, not just the test methods for which NVLAP can accredit. In addition, the applicant laboratory shall satisfy other laboratory and business requirements as specified by GSA.

All laboratories applying for the 17GSAP testing shall:

- first, achieve accreditation by NVLAP as a Basic Cryptographic and Security Testing (17BCS) laboratory and as a Cryptographic Algorithm Validation Testing (17CAV); and

- second, achieve accreditation by NVLAP as a NPIVP Testing Laboratory, in both 17PIV/01 and 17PIV/02 test methods.

D.3.2   Additional activities prior to an on-site assessment

There are no requirements additional to those provided in clause 3.2 of this handbook.

D.3.3   Additional on-site assessment requirements

There are no requirements additional to those provided in clause 3.3 of this handbook.

D.3.4   Additional proficiency testing requirements

D.3.4.1   General

NVLAP, in collaboration with all CST validation programs, considers the validation reports submitted to the validation programs as ongoing proficiency tests. A large number of flaws in the reports submitted to any of the validation programs can trigger the laboratory's suspension or revocation of the accreditation. For more information see 3.10 of this handbook.

D.3.4.2   Additional proficiency testing requirements for the 17GSAP testing

Proficiency testing for the 17GSAP tests will require proof of the laboratory's competence to set up and configure a testing hardware and software environment as instructed in the test, to use a PIV card(s) (with T=0 and/or T=1 protocols) and a PIV card reader, to perform all the operations instructed in the test (e.g., electronically personalize the card(s), generate key pair(s), generate and load personalized data objects, authenticate the card holder), and to run the tests as instructed.

D.4   Additional management requirements for accreditation

There are no requirements additional to those provided in clause 4 of this handbook.

D.5   Additional technical requirements for accreditation

D.5.1   General

There are no requirements additional to those provided in Section 5.1 of this handbook.

D.5.2   Additional personnel requirements

D.5.2.1   General

For a laboratory to qualify for accreditation under the CST LAP, the laboratory shall demonstrate, in addition to the technical expertise required by each test method as described below, that their personnel has basic knowledge of cryptographic and security practice for information systems and that the laboratory is aware of the governing standards and publications, especially the ones listed in this handbook.

D.5.2.2   Additional personnel requirements for the for the 17PIV and 17GSAP testing

The laboratory's personnel shall have experience or be trained prior to accreditation in the areas of:

a)   cryptography - symmetric versus asymmetric algorithms and uses;

b)   cryptography - encryption protocols and implementations;

c)   key management techniques and concepts;

d)   cryptographic self-test techniques;

e)   familiarity with the families of cryptographic algorithms;

f)   FIPS-approved and NIST-recommended security functions (FIPS 140-2 or successors);

g)   cryptography - Public Key Infrastructure (PKI);

h)   access control security models;

i)   smart cards;

j)   smart card readers (contact and contactless);

k)   Application Protocol Data Unit (APDU);

l)   Basic Encoding Rules (BER);

m)   biometric authentication techniques;

n)   concepts of the operational PIV systems;

o)   contact and contactless interface standards; and

p)   Server-based Certificate Validation Protocol (SCVP).

D.5.3   Additional accommodation and environmental conditions

The laboratory shall have appropriate areas, including ventilation and safety, for the use of test methods using chemical solvents and heating/cooling apparatus.

D.5.4   Additional test and calibration methods and method validation

There are no requirements additional to those provided in 5.4.

D.5.5   Additional equipment requirement for the 17GSAP testing

Supplemental to the additional equipment requirements listed for 17PIV testing (section C.5.5.2), the laboratory applying for accreditation for the 17GSAP testing shall also meet the following minimum hardware, software and operating system requirements for any platform on which the *PIV Data Model Tester* (SP800-85B) and the *Test Fixture Software* tools required for GSAP testing will run:

a) Hardware:

    1) at least 1 USB and 1 serial port available on the Windows XP test computer;

    2) Golden Contact PIV Card Reader - Gemalto GemPC twin USB HW111459A[1];

    3) Breakout Box - For connecting physical access readers - for additional information see GSA Laboratory Specification, section 3.3.4.3 - latest version from http://fips201ep.cio.gov/. The USB and Serial Communication cables from the breakout box will be connected to the IBM-compatible PC system;

    4) 22 AWG Wire - category 5 or similar Ethernet; and

    5) tools needed for the breakout box:
- Drill,
- Screw driver,
- Glue.

b) Software:

    1) BouncyCastle crypto provider, version 1.32 (bcprov-jdk15-132.jar) - available from http://www.bouncycastle.org/download/bcprov-jdk15-132.jar;

    2) BouncyCastle mail utilities, version 1.32 (bcmail-jdk15-132.jar) - available from http://www.bouncycastle.org/download/bcmail-jdk15-132.jar;

    3) Crpto++ DLL version 5.2.3 - available from http://www.cryptopp.com;

    4) *PIV Test Data Software* (which includes the *JPIV Test Data Generator* jar file and the *PIV Data Loader* executable) provided by NIST/ITL website http://csrc.nist.gov/piv-program - latest release available;

    5) unless otherwise specified by NVLAP on the CST LAP website, a *Gemplus GemPIV applet* v1.01 on Gemplus GemCombi Xpresso R4 E72K Smart Card (to be used when a "Golden Class A PIV Card" (PIVcard-ClassA) or "Golden T=0 PIV Card" or "PIVcard-T0" will be referred);

    6) unless otherwise specified by NVLAP on the CST LAP website, a *PIV EP v.108 Java Card Applet* on Oberthur ID-One Cosmo v5 64K Smart Card - to be used when a "Golden T=1 PIV Card" or "PIVcard-T1" will be referred;

    7) card reader driver provided by the manufacturer;

    8) SP 800-85B Data Conformance Test Tool v6.2.0 - Used to test data model conformance for a populated PIV Card. Available from http://fips201ep.cio.gov/tools.php;

    9) Cardholder Facial Image Test Tool v1.0.1 – Used to test the conformance of the PIV Facial Image to the specifications of SP 800-76-1 and INCITS 385. Available from http://fips201ep.cio.gov/tools.php;

    10) SCVP Client Test Tool v2.0.0 – A client application that interacts (using the RFC 5055 as the protocol) with the GSA Central Certificate Validator (CCV) service in order to determine validity for any given PIV Certificate using PKI-based path discovery and validation. Available from http://fips201ep.cio.gov/tools.php; and

    11) Data Populator Tool v2.3.0 - Used to randomly generate conformant data and load them on the PIV Card. Available from http://fips201ep.cio.gov/tools.php.

---

[1] Certain commercial entities, equipment, or materials may be identified in this document in order to describe a requirement adequately. Such identification is not intended to imply recommendation or endorsement by NIST.

D.5.6   Additional measurement traceability

D.5.6.1   Additional general requirements

There are no requirements additional to those provided in 5.6.1 of this handbook.

D.5.6.2   Additional calibration requirements

There are no requirements additional to those provided in 5.6.2 of this handbook.

D.5.6.3   Additional testing requirements for the 17GSAP testing

Laboratories shall use the test methods listed at the website http://fips201ep.cio.gov/contact.php under the "Test Procedures."

Prior to testing the IUT, the laboratory shall create an inventory list with all the equipment received and tag all systems. The IUT shall be NPIVP-certified before being considered for the GSA EP conformance testing, as the NPIVP is a prerequisite to the GSAP program.

During the conformance testing, the laboratory shall use and complete the following documentation:

- Approval Procedure;
- Test Procedures; and
- Evaluation Report.

The core function of a GSAP laboratory is to analyze and evaluate the IUT for conformance with FIPS 201 specifications. Based on the laboratory evaluation results, an authorized GSA official, the Approval Authority, makes the final determination as to whether the IUT should be approved.

Annex E

(normative)

Security Content Automation Protocol Testing

E.1   Additional general information

Please see E.2.3 for references to additional information regarding SCAP.

E.2   Scope of accreditation, test methods, additional references, terms and definitions

E.2.1   Scope of accreditation

NVLAP offers all interested laboratories a flexible, dynamic system of selecting a compound scope of accreditation under the CST LAP that best fits the laboratory's level of expertise and equipment.

The minimum level of required expertise is described as "Basic Cryptographic and Security (17BCS)" testing and is considered the foundation of all test methods covered under the CST LAP. The Basic Cryptographic and Security (17BCS) testing scope is not a stand-alone scope and it is mandated as a prerequisite for all test methods

E.2.2   Test methods

For each testing program, the test methods are listed below. When a hierarchically higher test method is elected, all test methods associated with the prerequisite scopes also become mandatory.

The SCAP testing is comprised of six test methods for the testing of the six component standards within SCAP, and a test suite (17SCAP/07) for the six components used in conjunction with, and for the specific capabilities.

17SCAP/01   Common Vulnerabilities and Exposures (CVE)

17SCAP/02   Common Configuration Enumeration (CCE)

17SCAP/03   Common Platform Enumeration (CPE)

17SCAP/04   Common Vulnerability Scoring System (CVSS)

17SCAP/05   eXtensible Configuration Checklist Document Format (XCCDF)

17SCAP/06   Open Vulnerability Assessment Language (OVAL)

17SCAP/07   Security Content Automation Protocol (SCAP)

E.2.3   Additional references for the Security Content Automation Protocol Testing (17SCAP)

E.2.3.1   NIST Special Publications (SP) for SCAP

— NIST SP 800-40: Creating a Patch and Vulnerability Management Program, version 2 or later
(see http://csrc nist.gov/publications/PubsSPs html)

— NIST SP 800-100: Information Security Handbook: A Guide for Managers
(see http://csrc nist.gov/publications/PubsSPs html)

— NIST SP 800-117: Guide to Adopting and Using the Security Content Automation Protocol (SCAP)
(see http://csrc nist.gov/publications/PubsSPs html)

— NIST SP 800-126: The Technical Specification for the Security Content Automation Protocol
(see http://csrc nist.gov/publications/PubsSPs html)

E.2.3.2   Other references for SCAP

— Security Content Automation Protocol (SCAP) Derived Test Requirements
(see http://scap.nist.gov for latest version)

— Security Content Automation Protocol Testing Implementation Guidance
(see http://scap.nist.gov for latest version)

— The Common Vulnerability Scoring System (CVSS) and Its Applicability to Federal Agency
Systems, NIST IR-7435 (see http://scap nist.gov)

— Specification for the Extensible Configuration Checklist Description Format (XCCDF)
(see http://scap.nist.gov)

— Common Platform Enumeration (CPE) – Specification (see http://scap nist.gov)

— Common Vulnerabilities and Exposures (CVE) (see http://scap nist.gov)

— Common Configuration Enumeration (CCE) (see http://scap nist.gov)

— Open Vulnerability Assessment Language (OVAL) (see http://scap.nist.gov)

E.2.4   Additional terms and definitions

E.2.4.1
Common Configuration Enumeration (CCE)
Provides unique identifiers to system configuration issues in order to facilitate correlation of configuration data across multiple information sources and tools.

E.2.4.2
Common Platform Enumeration (CPE)
A structured naming scheme for information technology systems, platforms, and packages.

E.2.4.3
Common Vulnerabilities and Exposures (CVE)
A dictionary of publicly known information security vulnerabilities and exposures.

E.2.4.4
Common Vulnerability Scoring System (CVSS)
A system to provide a standardized method for measuring the impact of the IT vulnerabilities.

E.2.4.5
Open Vulnerability Assessment Language (OVAL)
An information security community standard that facilitates measuring a machine state, and is often used for vulnerability, configuration and patch checking.

E.2.4.6
eXtensible Configuration Checklist Document Format (XCCDF)
A specification language for writing security checklists, benchmarks, and related documents. An XCCDF document represents a structured collection of security configuration rules for one or more applications and/or systems.

E.3   Additional accreditation process requirements

E.3.1   Additional accreditation requirements

There are no requirements additional to those provided in clause 3.1 of this handbook.

E.3.2   Additional activities prior to an on-site assessment

There are no requirements additional to those provided in clause 3.2 of this handbook.

E.3.3   Additional on-site assessment requirements

There are no requirements additional to those provided in clause 3.3 of this handbook.

E.3.4   Additional proficiency testing requirements

NVLAP, in collaboration with all CST validation programs, considers the validation reports submitted to the validation programs as ongoing proficiency tests. A large number of flaws in the reports submitted to any of the validation programs can trigger the laboratory's suspension or revocation of the accreditation. For more information see 3.10 of this handbook.

Proficiency testing for the 17SCAP tests will require proof of the laboratory's competence to set up and configure a testing hardware and software environment as instructed in the test. Using a sample artifact provided by NIST/CSD, the laboratory shall determine which test requirements are appropriate for the provided artifact, conduct the test procedures associated with those requirements, verify the results, and generate a report indicating the proposed validation status of the artifact.

E.4   Additional management requirements for accreditation

There are no requirements additional to those provided in clause 4 of this handbook.

E.5   Additional technical requirements for accreditation

E.5.1   General

There are no requirements additional to those provided in Section 5.1 of this handbook.

E.5.2   Additional personnel requirements

For a laboratory to qualify for accreditation under the CST LAP, the laboratory shall demonstrate, in addition to the technical expertise required by each test method as described below, that their personnel has basic knowledge of cryptographic and security practice for information systems and that the laboratory is aware of the governing standards and publications, especially the ones listed in this handbook.

The laboratory personnel shall have experience or be trained prior to accreditation in:

a) basic knowledge of vulnerability and configuration management (NIST SP 800-40 v2 or later and NIST SP 800-100);

b) basic knowledge of XML and how to read XML documents (W3C Extensible Markup Language (XML) 1.1 (Second Edition) or later);

c) familiarity with all SCAP standards (CVE, CCE, CPE, CVSS, XCCDF, OVAL including NIST SP 800-126) – latest versions (for more information see http://scap.nist.gov); and

d) familiarity with the Windows XP, Windows Vista, and Windows 7 operating systems.

E.5.3   Additional accommodation and environmental conditions

The laboratory shall have appropriate areas, including ventilation and safety, for the use of test methods using chemical solvents and heating/cooling apparatus.

E.5.4   Additional test and calibration methods and method validation

There are no requirements additional to those provided in 5.4.

E.5.5   Additional equipment requirements

The laboratory applying for accreditation for the 17SCAP testing shall be equipped with the following minimum hardware, software and operating system requirements:

a) Hardware:

1) Any IT system capable of properly executing Windows XP SP 2/3, Windows Vista SP2, Windows 7 and a domain controller such as Windows Server.
    i.   This can be a real system or supported through virtualization architecture.
    ii. Must be capable of executing the product under test as indicated by the documentation accompanying the product or as otherwise specified by the vendor of the product.

b) Software:[1]

1) Windows XP SP 2/3 and Windows Vista SP2 running on the IT system.
    i.   For FDCC and USGCB testing, the operating system must be configured to the correspond.
    ii. The OS must have Internet Explorer version 7 installed for Windows XP/Vista, and Internet Explorer version 8 for Windows 7.
    iii. The OS must be able to be joined to a test domain.

2) XML schema validation tool. The tester must be able to perform XML schema validation against XML results produced by the product under test.
    i.   The tool must be able to reference NIST provided schemas.

3) SCAP Reference Implementation
    i.   Requires Java Runtime Environment (JRE) version 1.5 or later.

4) XML viewer
    i.   This is necessary to review XML input and output files for comparison to expected results.

5) Access to the official NIST CVSS calculator, located at http://nvd.nist.gov/cvss.cfm?calculator&version=2.

6) Access to the National Vulnerability Database at http://nvd.nist.gov.

E.5.6   Additional measurement traceability

E.5.6.1   Additional general requirements

There are no requirements additional to those provided in 5.6.1 of this handbook.

E.5.6.2   Additional calibration requirements

There are no requirements additional to those provided in 5.6.2 of this handbook.

E.5.6.3   Additional testing requirements

There are no requirements additional to those provided in 5.6.3 of this handbook.

---

[1] Certain commercial entities, equipment, or materials may be identified in this document in order to describe a requirement adequately. Such identification is not intended to imply recommendation or endorsement by NIST.

Annex F

(informative)

Acronyms and abbreviations

The following acronyms and abbreviations are used throughout this handbook:

ANSI:	American National Standards Institute
APDU:	Application Protocol Data Unit
BCS:	Basic Cryptographic and Security
BER:	Basic Encoding Rules
CAVP:	Cryptographic Algorithm Validation Program
CAVS:	Cryptographic Algorithm Validation System
CCE:	Common Configuration Enumeration
CHUID:	Card Holder Unique Identifier
CMT LAP:	Cryptographic Module Testing Laboratory Accreditation Program
CMVP:	Cryptographic Module Validation Program
CPE:	Common Platform Enumeration
CSD:	Computer Security Division
CSEC:	Communications Security Establishment Canada
CST LAP:	Cryptographic and Security Testing Laboratory Accreditation Program
CVE:	Common Vulnerabilities and Exposures
CVSS:	Common Vulnerability Scoring System
DMM:	Digital Multi-Meter
DTR:	Derived Test Requirements
DVM:	Digital Voltmeter
FIPS:	Federal Information Processing Standard
GB:	Gigabytes
GSA EP:	General Service Administration Evaluation Program
GSAP:	General Service Administration Precursor
IEC:	International Electrotechnical Commission
IG:	Implementation Guidance
INCITS:	InterNational Committee for Information Technology Standards
ISO:	International Organization for Standardization
ITL:	Information Technology Laboratory

IUT:	Implementation-Under-Test
JRE:	Java Runtime Environment
MB:	Megabytes
NPIVP:	NIST Personal Identity Verification Program
NVLAP:	National Voluntary Laboratory Accreditation Program
OVAL:	Open Vulnerability Assessment Language
PIV:	Personal Identity Verification
PKI:	Public Key Infrastructure
QM:	Quality Manual
SCAP:	Security Content Automation Protocol
SP:	Special Publication
USB:	Universal Serial Bus
VCS:	Version Control System
VHD:	Virtual Hard Disk
VM:	Virtual Machine
VOM:	Volt-Ohm-Meter
XCCDF:	eXtensible Configuration Checklist Document Format

www.ingramcontent.com/pod-product-compliance
Lightning Source LLC
Chambersburg PA
CBHW060459060326
40689CB00020B/4584